WHICH? WAY TO CLEAN IT

CASSANDRA KENT

CONSUMERS' ASSOCIATION

Which? Books are commissioned and researched by
The Association for Consumer Research
and published by
Consumers' Association,
2 Marylebone Road, London NW1 4DF

Distributed by The Penguin Group:
Penguin Books Ltd, 27 Wrights Lane, London W8 5TZ

First published September 1994
Copyright © 1994 Consumers' Association Ltd

British Library Cataloguing in Publication Data
Kent, Cassandra
  Which? Way to Clean it. – (Which?
  Consumer Guides)
  I. Title II. Series
  648

ISBN 0 85202 550 5

Cover photographs by MC Picture Library
Typographic design by Paul Saunders
Typeset by Saxon Graphics Limited, Derby
Printed and bound by Firmin-Didot (France), Group Herissey, No d'impression: 27885

WHICH? WAY TO CLEAN IT

ABOUT THE AUTHOR

Cassandra Kent is a freelance journalist, author and broadcaster specialising in consumer affairs and home management.

She worked for *Which?* magazine, a broadcasting trade union and the Family Planning Association before joining *Good Housekeeping*, where she worked for some years, including a period as a Director of Research and Testing of the Good Housekeeping Institute. She now writes for magazines and newspapers and is author of over twenty practical household books.

CONTENTS

INTRODUCTION

*W*hich? *Way to Clean It* saves you time and trouble when you are cleaning your home and your possessions, while helping you to achieve the best results. Gone, fortunately, are the days when cleaning played a major part in many people's lives. Today, with the assistance of electrical equipment and technologically advanced products, cleaning is no longer a major chore.

However, it still has to be done. How often and how much is your choice. If the members of your household are out a good deal, things should not get too dirty. Encourage everyone to put their clothes and belongings away every day, leaving the decks clear for cleaning. Try to recruit their help in cleaning, too. A weekly whip-round with the vacuum cleaner, duster and appropriate kitchen and bathroom products should maintain a perfectly acceptable level of cleanliness.

If your home is occupied most of the time, particularly if there are young children around, you will undoubtedly spend more time cleaning. The washing, in particular, will be a bigger task. This book gives you easy-reference instructions on everything from getting tomato ketchup stains out of clothes to restoring cricket whites to their former glory.

Starting from the premise that most people do not find cleaning the most enjoyable or fulfilling activity in their lives, this book shows how to establish a manageable routine and tells you which are the most effective products for cleaning specific items or materials – everything from chandeliers to sheepskin rugs. No more disasters with shrunken garments, damaged antiques or streaky windows! No more wasted time, slaving away with ineffective products and equipment.

Knowing when you can get away with the bare minimum and when a more thorough job is needed is one of the keys to a time-saving cleaning routine. Preventing your home and possessions from becoming very dirty in the first place is another.

Many people tend to come unstuck when it comes to cleaning items made from unfamiliar materials – carpets and laminated worktops are probably not a problem for them but vellum lampshades and bronze cutlery might be neglected simply because they are unsure about the best method of cleaning them.

In brief, this book tells you how often you need to clean things, what product to use and how to use it most efficiently. It is divided into parts which deal with different areas of the home, the garden, your possessions and even your pets. Cross-references make it easy to find the section you want at a glance, and each part is dotted with boxes containing cleaning tips. The brand-name directory lists products which are available for specific purposes. Some of these are not easy to find on the high street, and in the case of products which are available only from one supplier, addresses are supplied. The Addresses section at the back of the book also provides the names of trade organisations, specialist manufacturers and services.

Keeping things clean is not a science or an art; it is a way of maintaining order and comfort in your home, ensuring items of value do not deteriorate through neglect and creating a pleasant ambience for those who live in and visit your home. How much or how little you choose to clean will depend on you.

Which? Way to Clean It takes the mystique out of cleaning. The Guide also tells you what you *should* do and what you should not do – the latter probably more important than the former. Tales of carpets with irredeemably stained patches and baths with permanently stained enamel are legion. Anything you care about or believe is valuable is best entrusted to the hands of an expert unless you are absolutely sure how to handle it. Think clean, but do not become a slave to cleanliness. Your time and effort are valuable commodities in themselves, so take advantage of every labour-saving, time-efficient product available.

1

ORGANISING YOUR CLEANING

Basic household cleaning
Essential cleaning products
Setting up a cleaning file
Cleaning tools
Cleaning routines
Storing cleaners
Hiring help with cleaning

BASIC HOUSEHOLD CLEANING

Keeping your home clean need not be an endless, time-consuming, back-breaking chore; gone are the days of black-leading grates, brushing stairs on hands and knees and beating rugs with wooden sticks.

Nowadays, there is a product or appliance to clean almost everything in your home, and although manufacturers would like you to believe that all their cleaning products are essential, all you really need are some key items.

This book will tell you what products to use, how to clean things as easily as possible and how to organise your cleaning to save yourself time and energy. Work out a routine that suits you and stick to it. Do not panic if you sometimes skip cleaning; dust is only a worry if you or someone in your family suffer from asthma or an allergy to house dust. Most importantly for health, keep kitchens and lavatories clean.

ESSENTIAL CLEANING PRODUCTS

The absolute basics for most homes are:

- washing-up liquid
- mild household detergent
- abrasive household detergent
- biological washing powder
- specialist metal cleaners
- furniture polish
- a selection of soapflakes and detergents for laundry.

It is also useful to keep ammonia, white spirit, turpentine, laundry borax, bicarbonate of soda, bleach, methylated spirit, washing soda and white vinegar in stock as they can be combined to clean a vast number of household surfaces.

SETTING UP A CLEANING FILE

A cleaning file can save hours of frustration, especially for those items which rarely need cleaning, but which need to be cleaned in a particular way using specialist products. Put laundering and cleaning instructions for all your upholstery, furniture, surfaces, household items and clothes in a ring binder so that you can refer to them quickly. Keep a note of any successful stain removal or cleaning treatments. You do not need to be very organised about the file as long as you throw the instructions into it when you buy something new.

If you are moving into a new home where the cooker and carpets are being left, try to get care information from the departing owners before they leave – and file it. Most of the time you will not need to refer to the file but the information will be there should you need it.

CLEANING TOOLS

There is no need to cram your cupboard full of every cleaning gadget in existence. Most household tasks can be tackled with a few items and you should only invest in more specialised equipment if it proves necessary.

The basic tools for your cleaning routine should be:

Essential equipment

- vacuum cleaner
- hard-/soft-bristled brooms
- dustpan with hard-/soft-bristled brushes
- lavatory brush and holder
- cellulose sponges (old loofahs make excellent cleaning pads)
- squeegee floor mop and bucket
- buckets and bowls
- dusters and polishing cloths
- a couple of chamois leathers
- washing-up utensils

- household gloves – keep separate pairs for specific tasks such as washing-up, lavatory-cleaning etc.
- a nose and mouth mask to prevent inhalation of fumes given off by certain cleaning products.

> **If your fingernails are long, rubber gloves will last longer if you turn them inside out and stick a small piece of waterproof plaster in each fingertip.**

CLEANING ROUTINES

Following a simple routine is the most effective way of maintaining cleanliness. Divide your home and its contents into three or four categories: things that need daily cleaning (surfaces and items used most frequently), things that need regular cleaning, things that need occasional cleaning and things which require a once-yearly blitz.

You will save yourself time and effort by maintaining a routine and not allowing things to get so dirty that cleaning them is a huge and tedious job. Save major cleaning for when you have time to complete it.

Recruit a family member or friend to help; it will take far less time if you work together. For example, if your helper empties cupboards and washes the contents, you can simultaneously be cleaning out the cupboards themselves and putting things back.

Daily cleaning   Lavatories and kitchen surfaces should be cleaned daily. Try to wash up, tidy the kitchen and wipe over all the work surfaces once a day with a cleaner that contains a bactericide – this should keep germs at bay. If you have pets that walk on worktops (this should not be encouraged) you should always prepare food on chopping boards that are stored away from where they walk. (See Pets, Part 7.)

It takes at least half an hour for the moisture lost by bodies overnight to evaporate, so air and make beds before you go out in the morning. Ideally, you should strip the bed when you get up and make it after breakfast. Try to make sure everyone in your home does the same – it automatically makes bedrooms look tidier and cleaner.

Start by ventilating the room you are going to clean. Closed windows provide insulation and keep out intruders but they also allow smells to build up, and household pests love to breed in the hot humid atmosphere produced by central heating. Research has shown that there are far more allergens in most homes than are found outside.

Regular cleaning

Next, tidy the room. Throw out dead flowers, clean ashtrays, remove dirty cups and put things back in their right place. If this is all you have time to do, the room will at least *look* cleaner.

When the room is ventilated close the windows before you start cleaning. Sweep or vacuum first as this tends to raise dust. Then dust surfaces and ornaments, applying polish or another cleaning product if needed. Start dusting on one side of a door and work round the room until you reach the other side; in this way no section will be missed. If you are interrupted by the doorbell or a telephone call put your dusters down where you are and you will know where to start again. Always dust higher surfaces first as some dust will fall on to lower ones.

WASHING FLOORS

Use two buckets when you wash a floor. Fill one with the cleaning solution, the other with clear warm water. Wet your squeegee mop in the cleaning solution and wash a section of the floor. Rinse the mop in the clean water before putting it back in the cleaning solution. In this way you will not be washing the floor with dirty water. Change the rinsing water as necessary.

***Special
cleaning***

How often a room needs a really good turn-out depends on the general wear-and-tear to your home. If your regular cleaning routine is reasonably well maintained it will not be very often, but neglecting things for too long results in more work later on.

Use the opportunity of a major turn-out to take down curtains for cleaning, shampoo the carpet and upholstery and clean the walls, windows and so on.

Go through cupboards and drawers and dispose of items which you no longer use.

Mend or take to a professional anything which needs repairing or cleaning.

Tackle one room at a time and do not move to another until you have finished the first. Even if you have set aside some days for the task it is almost impossible to maintain the impetus to wash, say, the walls in six rooms. You will feel much more positive if you complete one room at a time.

BROOM CARE

Wash broom and brush bristles from time to time in a solution of washing-up liquid. Rinse in warm water and then in cold salty water to stiffen the bristles. Hang brooms up by their handles (screw a hook on the end if necessary), as the bristles will be flattened if you stand the broom on them.

STORING CLEANERS

- Try to keep all your cleaning gear in one place. If your home is on several levels you may want to have a cleaning cache on each floor to save carting stuff around – this may be more expensive initially but the cost evens out.

- Do not decant cleaning products into other containers without labelling them clearly and ineradicably.
- Use an old shopping basket or a plastic box to carry your kit around with you while you clean. This saves lots of journeys back and forth.
- Clean your cleaning equipment before you put it away. Check that fluff and hairs are removed from vacuum cleaner attachments, brooms and brushes. Wash dirt and grit out of buckets. Wash or discard dusters and polishing cloths that have become too dirty to re-use.

DIRT-DEFYING DUSTER

Make a dirt-defying duster by soaking it in an equal mixture of paraffin and vinegar for a couple of hours. Wring it out and allow to dry naturally before using. Impregnating the duster with oil and acid allows it to pick up dust rather than just spreading it around. Store in a lidded container when not in use, and make sure the duster is clean before you start.

BUYING A VACUUM CLEANER –
A CHECKLIST

- Does it run smoothly?

- Is it the right height for you?

- Are the attachments easy to fit?

- Does it suit your home (i.e. the amount of space, stairs and types of surfaces)?

- If you suffer from allergies or asthma, is the vacuum cleaner designed to eliminate more dust than standard models?

- Does it have a retractable cable or other means of storing the cable neatly?

Type of vacuum cleaner	Good points	Bad points
Upright	Good beating action. Covers large areas fast. Suction can be set to clean hard floors.	Not good at getting into corners or under low furniture. Not convenient for stairs. Not suitable for loop-pile carpets.
Cylinder	Flexible hose ideal for stairs and for getting under furniture. Good for cleaning upholstery and curtains.	Flexible hose can kink. Trailing the cleaner behind you can be cumbersome.
Multipurpose	Cleans carpets and hard floors. Can be used to shampoo carpets, and can vacuum up water.	Bulky to store. Expensive. Can be noisy.
Hand-held cordless	Good for cars, carpet edges, cupboards and picking up crumbs.	Needs recharging after a few minutes of vacuuming. No good for large surfaces.
Miniature	Suitable for cars, hobby work and home office equipment.	Not designed for domestic use, very small capacity.

ATTACHMENTS

Making maximum use of vacuum cleaner attachments will eliminate a lot of manual dusting. You can use them to clean walls, curtains, upholstery, glazed pictures, mirrors and so on.

The *crevice tool* can reach awkward areas and clean right up to the skirting boards.

The *upholstery tool* is for soft surfaces, curtains, mattresses and some stairs.

The *soft round dusting brush* is for cleaning picture rails, dado rails, bannisters and carved wood.

HIRING HELP WITH CLEANING

Hiring someone else to clean for you only relieves you of the chore if you are cautious about whom you appoint.

Think first about how much help you need. For a small home, three to four hours a week should be enough for routine cleaning plus a few extra non-regular tasks such as polishing silver, cleaning an oven or cleaning windows. A larger home may need more time and if you have a messy household you may prefer to have fewer hours more frequently, in order to keep chaos at bay.

Alternatively, you may just want an occasional blitz or spring-clean, in which case your best bet is to find a reliable local agency which will send round a team or individual to give your home a thorough clean-out. This is useful if dirt has got a grip and you want things like paintwork washed, light switches cleaned, kitchen cupboards turned out and so on. It can also be a lifesaver if you have got people coming to stay or want to return from holiday to find everything squeaky clean.

The best way to find help with cleaning is to ask around and advertise locally. Rely on personal recommendation if you can, having made searching   ***Finding a cleaner*** enquiries about the two most important factors – honesty and cleaning ability. If you are considering someone without personal recommendation ask if he or she has worked for someone else and whether you can take up a telephone reference. Try to check that the referee is not a friend or relative of the applicant. If you have any concerns, look elsewhere.

Otherwise use an agency to find help for you. Agencies either charge a fee for finding the cleaner, who is then paid by you, or charge a slightly higher-than-average hourly rate if they employ the cleaner. Many people think the higher rate is worth paying as the agency will handle any problems which occur, sacking the individual or finding a replacement if misdemeanours are committed or he or she is otherwise unsatisfactory.

When interviewing, show your potential employee all round your home and spell out exactly what you want done; make sure he or she is happy to do it. Many cleaners have unfavourite tasks like cleaning ovens or insides of windows and if these chores are high on your list of priorities you will want to hire someone who is prepared to undertake them.

If you are hiring someone yourself make it quite clear what the hourly rate for the job will be. Also discuss whether you will provide some paid holiday (specifying the number of days) and what will happen if your cleaning day falls on a public holiday. Normally, domestic cleaners are self-employed and you do not need to provide a written contract of employment. An oral agreement is sufficient. The cleaner would then be paid in cash or by cheque each time he or she worked for you. If you are taking on a cleaner as your employee, and you will be paying their National Insurance and income tax, you must provide a written contract containing the terms and conditions of employment. To find out about the National Insurance and income tax costs involved consult your local Inland Revenue office. Next, decide whether you will let the cleaner have a key, to allow access to your home when you are not in. It is worth bearing in mind that even if you are sure that your cleaner is scrupulously honest other members of his or her household may not be and may take advantage of the trust placed in your cleaner. If you do allow someone to have keys to your home, inform your household insurers otherwise you may have problems claiming in the event of burglary.

Note, too, that if you have a burglar alarm you will have to ensure that your cleaner can switch it off – again, this is information which you may prefer to restrict to members of your household.

You should in any case inform your household contents insurers that you are employing someone to clean your home. This should not affect the premium although, oddly enough, insurers are more concerned about people who are in your home for long periods (e.g. a cleaner who comes in every morning) than if you just employ someone for a couple of hours a week. Their theory is that the longer people are in your home the greater the opportunity they have to steal things.

You should also tell the company that insures the building that you employ a cleaner in case it requires you to take out a policy for accidental damage caused by the cleaner. Also make sure you are covered in the event of your cleaner being injured while on your premises.

Keeping standards up

If you can find good help with cleaning you will save yourself time and trouble. But it is important to keep your cleaner up to the mark; if the standard of work drops significantly without good reason you should point this out. It is also a good idea to vary the chores you set each time so that the routine does not become repetitive and dull for the cleaner. Obviously some areas (kitchen, bathrooms, etc.) need regular attention but you can vary other chores so that one week metal is polished, the next all the curtains are vacuumed, and so on.

You should also try to ensure that you are getting the time you pay for. If you cannot be at home yourself perhaps a friend could occasionally pop in to see that the cleaner has not left early or is spending time on the telephone at your expense.

Checking up in this way may seem excessively cautious, but the fact is that you are employing someone to help you and make your life easier and there is a contract between you and your cleaner, verbal or written, that confirms what both parties have agreed. In a business situation people do not put up with staff working shorter hours than specified or spending time on personal phone calls or coffee breaks. It is not unreasonable, since you are paying for your cleaner's time, to expect value for money and a professional attitude to the job.

Au pairs

You can have some help with cleaning if you employ an au pair, although the Home Office lays down regulations about the number of hours and specifies 'light household duties' only.

Au pairs must be single and aged between 17 and 27. They can come from a number of countries specified by the Home Office (see box below). If you employ someone from one of these countries or elsewhere abroad full-time he or she must have a work permit.

Au pairs may not work more than five hours a day and any child-minding should be included in this total. They should also not be asked to scrub filthy floors or undertake major cleaning tasks. However, tidying up, vacuuming, dusting and polishing are all considered light duties.

Au pairs from the following countries can work in the UK: all members of the EC, Andorra, Bosnia Herzegovina, Croatia, Cyprus, Czech Republic, Faeroes, Greenland, Hungary, Liechtenstein, Macedonia, Malta, Monaco, San Marino, Slovak Republic, Slovenia, Switzerland and Turkey.

AVOIDING COWBOY CONTRACTORS

Employing a cleaning contractor for a particular job requires vigilance. High unemployment has encouraged many unqualified people to set themselves up as carpet cleaners, upholstery cleaners, curtain cleaners, dry-cleaners and so on. They may well have satisfactory equipment but they may lack training, expertise and awareness of certain problems.

Do not ever use a cleaning contractor who is either not a member of a recognised trade body or does not come with personal recommendation from someone whose opinion you trust.

Tales are legion of carpets ruined with rust marks because foil wasn't put under furniture legs, upholstery ripped to shreds by steam-cleaning and designer clothes spoiled by incompetent dry-cleaning.

Under Addresses (Part 12) are listed some trade organisations which vet their potential members and which operate a code of practice, usually drawn up in conjunction with the Office of Fair Trading. In the event of an unsatisfactory piece of work being carried out they will send round inspectors and arbitrate between the client and the contractor. This may not always produce a perfect situation from the client's point of view but it is a lot better than responding to a special-offer cleaning leaflet pushed through your letterbox whose operator, after the work is done, turns out to be a fly-by-night with a PO box address who will never reply to your complaint.

Carpets, upholstery and so on are expensive items which need care in cleaning. If you have any concerns about someone who offers to do a job for you, don't use that firm.

STAINS BEFORE CLEANING

Tackling stains is the first step in many cleaning processes. Stains become more difficult or even impossible to get out when they are not treated correctly. For example, hot water 'sets' some stains, such as blood, which may then always remain visible.

It makes sense to keep a stain removal kit in the cupboard and use the items in it only for this purpose. Otherwise, the day you want nail varnish-remover you will find the bottle in the bedroom has run out.

Buy stain removers in small quantities and replace them as needed. If you decant something into another container (not advisable with some chemicals), make sure it is clearly labelled and in a suitable bottle. Products which are sold in glass containers should not be decanted into plastic.

BASIC KIT FOR STAIN REMOVAL

Acetone (also sold as non-oily nail varnish-remover)
Ammonia
Biological detergent (also called enzyme detergent)
Bleach
French chalk (fuller's earth or unperfumed talcum powder)
Glycerine
Grease solvents (sold in aerosol, liquid and stick form)
Hydrogen peroxide
Laundry borax
Methylated spirit
Pre-wash laundry products
Proprietary stain removers (these are specially formulated for particular stains such as ink, rust, tar, etc.)
Surgical spirit
Toothbrush or nailbrush
White spirit (paint-thinner)
White vinegar
White rags

White unpatterned kitchen paper
(See Directory at back of book for details of brand-name cleaning products.)

PROTECTIVE MEASURES

- Always follow the instructions supplied with a cleaning product, noting any surfaces on which it cannot be used.
- Never use coloured rags or paper napkins on stains – the chemicals can cause their colour to run.

- Always open a window or outside door so that the area is well ventilated. *When using stain removers*
- Wear suitable gloves to protect your hands.
- Avoid getting chemicals on your skin or in your eyes. If you do, rinse thoroughly with cold water. If stinging or burning persists see your doctor or go to the accident and emergency department ('casualty') of your nearest hospital.
- Keep all chemicals away from naked flames. Do not smoke while you are treating a stain.
- Keep children and pets out of the way while you are working. Treat stains away from aquarium fish and caged animals if possible.

TREATMENT TIPS

- Treat stains as soon as possible – early treatment is more likely to be successful.
- Test the cleaning product on an inconspicuous area before applying to the stain. This might be a patch of wallpaper that is always hidden by a picture or an inside seam of a garment.

- Never mix stain-removal treatments – the chemicals may react together adversely.
- It may be necessary to apply a stain remover several times. This is preferable to the 'blitz' approach – e.g. using a large quantity of bleach on something.
- Pay for professional cleaning if an item is valuable or if the manufacturer recommends it. If you have already tried to treat the stain, tell the cleaner what products you have used as this may affect how he treats the item.
- Keep care instructions in a ring binder or box file if you have removed them from the item to which they refer.

> **Initial treatment for any stain is to blot it with kitchen paper or an old white towel. Solid stains should be lifted off a surface using a blunt knife or the bowl of a spoon. Work carefully from the perimeter of the stain towards the centre to prevent it spreading.**

SPECIFIC STAIN TREATMENTS

Adhesives Treat by scraping up as much as possible and then use an appropriate solvent. Adhesives manufacturers produce solvents specifically designed to remove glue spills. Buy the solvent at the same time as the glue in case of spillage.

Carpets Stains on pile carpets which will not come off can be removed by snipping the pile slightly with very sharp embroidery scissors. This may be essential if a carpet has a built-in foam backing which could be dissolved by stain remover or solvent. Use non-oily nail varnish-remover on clear adhesives; use paint-thinner on epoxy resin; use liquid grease solvent on latex adhesive.

Hard surfaces Use white or methylated spirit to remove sticky label residue, except on bare metal, on which nail varnish-remover should do the trick. Allow latex adhesives to set, then roll them off with your finger.

Carpets Freshly spilled beer on carpets and washable fabrics should come out after being sponged with warm water or squirted from a soda syphon. Shampoo the whole carpet afterwards, or you may end up with a clean patch which is just as conspicuous as a stain. Use methylated spirit on old beer stains.

Beer

Soft furnishings and fabrics If normal washing fails, sponge white fabrics with 20-vol strength hydrogen peroxide in a solution of six parts cold water, and coloured fabrics with a solution of 30ml white vinegar in 500ml cold water.
Non-washable fabrics Use an aerosol dry-cleaner.

Washable fabrics Rinse thoroughly in cold water, then launder in a biological detergent solution. White fabrics such as table linen can be stretched over a bowl or basin, sprinkled with laundry borax and left for 15 minutes or so. Rinse with hot water and launder according to fabric.

Beetroot

Coloured fabric should be soaked in a warm solution of laundry borax (15ml to 500ml water).

Scrape up with a spoon, then sponge with warm water or a laundry borax solution.

Bird droppings

Carpets You may need to use a proprietary stain remover.
Non-washable fabrics and upholstery Use an aerosol stain remover.
Washable fabrics Droppings which fall on laundry hanging out to dry should come out with a normal re-wash. Droppings which contain berry stains may need a solution of 20-vol hydrogen peroxide (one part to six parts cold water). On white fabrics use diluted bleach.

Blood   *Carpets* Spray the stain with a soda syphon, then sponge with plain cold water.

Washable fabrics Soak in cold water containing a handful of salt. Then soak in a solution of biological detergent and launder as usual.

Non-washable fabrics Sponge with a solution of ammonia (2.5ml to 1 litre cold water). Rinse with cold water and immediately pat dry with kitchen paper.

Blood on a mattress requires a thick paste of bicarbonate of soda (use as little water as possible). Stand the mattress on its side so that as little water as possible gets into it. When the paste is dry brush it off. Repeat this process until the stain goes. Finally, sponge with cold salty water.

Candle wax   *Hard surfaces* Scrape up as much as you can using the bowl of a spoon. Put a plastic bag of ice cubes on the wax to harden it, then chip it off. Take a medium-hot iron and apply it to the remains of the stain *over a piece of white blotting paper*. (You can use brown paper but it is less absorbent; kitchen paper is too thin and the heat from the iron may damage the surface below.)

On coloured candle stains, use a stain remover on fabrics and wall coverings and methylated spirit on carpets.

Car and cycle oil   Use white spirit on concrete garage floors and driveways. Use a solution of sugar soap on asphalt. See also page 157.

Carbon paper   Use either a stain remover or methylated spirit (but not on acetates or triacetates).

Chewing-gum   *Carpets and upholstery* Use a special chewing-gum remover (see Addresses section).

Clothes Fill a plastic bag with ice cubes or put the garment in the freezer (in a plastic bag) so that the gum hardens and can be chipped off. Use a liquid stain remover on any remaining marks. Launder or sponge with warm water.

Scrape up as much as possible.
Carpets, upholstery and non-washable fabrics Use a pro-prietary stain remover.
Washable fabrics Launder in biological detergent.

Chocolate

Carpets Blot up as much as possible, then squirt with a soda syphon and pat dry. This should remove fresh black coffee but white coffee leaves a grease mark which should be treated with a solution of carpet shampoo or a carpet spot removal kit. Dried coffee stains should be given the soda syphon treatment several times, allowing it to dry between applications.
Non-washable fabrics and upholstery Sponge first with laundry borax solution (15ml borax to 500ml warm water), then with clear water. Where marks persist, use a stain remover.
Washable fabrics Rinse in warm water then soak in a biological detergent solution or a laundry borax solution. Launder as usual and use a stain remover to lift any traces.

Coffee

Put the stained garments through another cycle, using a special dye remover designed for machine use. Soaking laundry in a biological detergent solution may help. A bleach solution will deal with white fabrics. (See Laundry, Part 5.)

Colour run in laundry load

Treat foundation cream, lipstick, eyeshadow and mascara with white spirit, then launder the items or sponge them with warm water.
    Spilled nail varnish should be blotted well, then removed with non-oily nail varnish-remover.

Cosmetics

Wallcoverings If the damage covers a smallish space the only solution is to fix a patch. Tear it to an irreg-ular shape so that the edges will not look quite so obvious. This is quite successful with patterned paper but tends to be a bit obvious with plain papers. On vinyl wallcoverings and bedheads use a household cleaner and rinse. Restore sheen by buff-ing well with a soft cloth.

Crayon

Creosote *Washable fabrics* Hold a pad of white cloth on top of the stain and dab liquid lighter fuel or eucalyptus oil from underneath to push the stain into the pad. Old stains should first be softened by covering with a solution of glycerine and warm water (equal parts) left on for an hour or so, then rinsed out. Launder according to fabric type.
Non-washable fabrics These should be dry-cleaned professionally. Call in a specialist carpet cleaner if necessary.

Curry Curry produces a tricky stain which should be removed professionally from garments or furnishings which you value. Otherwise scrape up as much as possible and treat as follows:
Carpets and non-washable fabrics Sponge with a laundry borax solution (15ml to 500ml warm water), then with clean water and pat dry. Treat remaining marks with a stain remover.
Washable fabrics Soak in warm water, changing it if necessary. Squeeze out as much water as possible and apply a solution of equal parts glycerine and warm water. Leave for at least an hour then rinse with clear water. Repeat if necessary. Launder using biological detergent. White items can be treated with a bleach solution.

Dyes *Carpets, non-washable fabrics and upholstery* Sponge with methylated spirit (not on acetates or triacetates) to which a few drops of household ammonia have been added. Repeat if necessary. Have valuable items dry-cleaned professionally. (See Dry-cleaning, Part 5.)
Hard surfaces Mop up immediately with a dry cloth. Do not use water as it will spread the dye. Dye which has dried in cannot be removed.
Washable fabrics Soak in a biological detergent solution, then launder as usual. On white washable fabrics use a proprietary dye stripper, following the instructions supplied. Silk and wool can be soaked in a 20-vol hydrogen peroxide solution (one part to

six parts cold water) for a maximum of 15 minutes. Rinse immediately and launder by hand.

Scrape up as much as possible, rubbing gently with kitchen paper to loosen the mark. Raw egg should be mopped up and then sponged with cold salty water.
Carpets Use a carpet spotting kit or proprietary stain remover, then shampoo the carpet. Use an aerosol stain remover on raw egg stains.
Non-washable fabrics and upholstery Sponge with cold salty water, then with plain water. Use an upholstery shampoo on any remaining marks.
Washable fabrics Soak in cold salty water, then rinse. Soak in plain water then launder. Raw egg should be removed using biological detergent.

Egg

See oil, fat and grease.

Fat

Fabrics and upholstery Dab flower stains with methylated spirit (not acetates or triacetates), sponge with warm water and, if possible, launder.
Wallcoverings Brush off as much as possible and use an aerosol or liquid stain remover applied with a cotton bud. Try to avoid flowerheads touching walls.
Vases and bowls Marks can be removed by soaking the vessel in a weak bleach solution for 30 minutes.

Flowers

Upholstery Use an aerosol stain remover or methylated spirit (not acetates and triacetates).
Fabric lampshades Brush thoroughly but gently with a soft brush, then use an aerosol stain remover.
Plastic and vellum lampshades Wipe with a cloth dampened in a solution of soapflakes. Sponge off with clear water and leave to dry.

Flying insects

Blot immediately with kitchen paper or a white towel.
Carpets and upholstery Sponge with warm water and then shampoo. Remaining colour stains should be dabbed with methylated spirits.

Fruit juices

Washable fabrics Rinse in cold running water. Stretch table and bed linen over a bowl or sink and pour hot water through the stain. Squeeze out water and cover marks with a glycerine solution (equal parts glycerine and warm water). Launder items according to their fabric.

Non-washable fabrics Sponge with cold water and allowed to dry naturally. Then use a proprietary stain remover.

Grass   *Washable fabrics* Stains should come out when the article is laundered. If marks remain, dab with methylated spirit (not acetates or triacetates) and rinse.

Non-washable fabrics Cover the stain with a mixture of cream of tartar powder and fine salt (equal parts), leave for 15 minutes and brush dry. Dry-clean.

Grease   See oil, fat and grease.

Hair oil   Tends to mark bedheads and wallcoverings.

Fabric-covered headboards Use a proprietary aerosol stain remover and once the stain is out treat with a protective spray.

Wooden headboards Oil will tend to sink in. Rub in the direction of the grain with a white cloth moistened in white spirit. Buff to a shine when the mark is gone.

Painted walls Use a household cleaner neat. Sponge the area with clear water.

Wallpaper Treat as for oil unless the paper is washable, in which case sponge with a weak solution of washing-up liquid then sponge with clear water and pat dry with kitchen paper.

Vinyl wallcoverings Use white spirit on bad marks. Then wipe over with a solution of household cleaner and rinse with clear water.

Hair spray   Will wash out of washable fabrics.

Non-washable fabrics Should be treated with a stain remover.

Mirrors Wipe with a cloth dampened with methylated spirit.

Scrape up as much as possible, then treat as follows: *Ice cream*
Carpets Wipe with a damp cloth, then use a carpet
spotting kit or shampoo the carpet. If grease marks
remain use a proprietary stain remover, first checking that the carpet is not foam-backed.
Non-washable fabrics Use a proprietary stain remover,
then bleach out any colour with a solution of 20-vol
hydrogen peroxide (one part to six parts cold water).
Washable fabrics Soak in a warm solution of biological detergent (use ordinary detergent if the fabric is
not suitable). Launder at the highest temperature
the fabric can take even if it means washing the
item on its own. Silk and wool should never be
soaked so sponge first with a warm solution of laundry borax (15ml to 500ml water) and immediately
afterwards with warm water.

Inks are difficult to remove and some old ink stains   *Inks*
will never come out of certain surfaces.
Carpets Ballpoint ink should be dried up as quickly
as possible using cotton buds and paper towel. Dab
with methylated spirit or use a proprietary stain
remover. Some ballpoint pen manufacturers recommend products for removing their ink, so if this
treatment does not work ask them for advice.
Fountain pen ink stains need squirting with a soda
syphon to dilute the stain then mopping with
kitchen paper or an old white towel. Make up a hot
solution of soapflakes and apply as a poultice on a
white fabric pad. Leave for at least 15 minutes, then
blot and repeat until the marks disappear. Rinse
with clear water. For bad marks use a carpet spotting kit and possibly a carpet shampoo.
  Blot felt-tip pen stains with cotton buds and
paper towel, then dab with methylated spirit.
Non-washable fabrics Use a proprietary stain remover
on felt-tip or fountain pen stains.
Washable fabrics White fabrics can be treated with
household bleach. Keep ink stains damp using cold
water until you have finished treatment. Dried ink
is much harder to remove.

Vinyl wallcoverings Scrub ballpoint ink stains with a stiff nailbrush dipped into a solution of washing-up liquid. Use a non-abrasive household cleaner on felt-tip pen marks, then clean with a solution of washing-up liquid and rinse off. Use an aerosol vinyl cleaner to restore shine.

Iron mould and rust marks

Washable fabrics Squirt or dab with lemon juice (any kind, including that sold in bottles or plastic containers) and cover with a thin layer of fine salt. Leave for an hour, rinse in cold water and launder as usual. Large white articles, such as sheets, which are heavily marked, can be washed using a dye remover.
Non-washable fabrics Treat persistent stains with a proprietary rust remover and then rinse or sponge it off.

Jam, chutney and other preserves

Scrape up as much as possible with the bowl of a spoon.
Carpets Wipe with a damp cloth several times then use a carpet shampoo. Coloured marks should be treated with methylated spirit.
Non-washable fabrics Sponge with a solution of washing-up liquid, blot dry with kitchen paper and repeat if necessary. Rinse with clear water. Any remaining marks should be covered with a layer of laundry borax powder, left for 15 minutes, then sponged. Otherwise use a proprietary stain remover.
Washable fabrics Items should be soaked in a laundry borax solution (15ml borax to 500ml warm water) before laundering.

Mayonnaise

Carpets and non-washable fabrics Wipe with a damp cloth, working into the stain to avoid spreading it. When dry use an aerosol stain remover. Carpets may need an application of shampoo.
Table linen and washable fabrics Sponge with warm water (hot will set the egg content and make it harder to remove). Soak in a biological detergent solution, then launder as usual.

Mayonnaise on expensive or 'difficult fabric' garments will need professional dry-cleaning.

Medicines

Sponge with warm water, then launder, using methylated spirit to remove any trace of colour. If a stain looks particularly sinister ask your local pharmacist what is in the medicine and how to treat the mark.

Metal polishes

Spoon and blot up as much as possible.
Carpets Dab the stain with methylated spirit and let it dry naturally. Beat with a stiff handbrush to loosen the powdery residue, then vacuum it up. Shampoo after vacuuming if necessary.
Washable fabrics Use a proprietary stain remover, then launder.
Non-washable fabrics Sponge and leave to dry then brush thoroughly with a stiff clothes-brush (which you will need to clean afterwards). Use a proprietary stain remover on any remaining marks.

Mildew

Mildew is a growth of spores which continue to develop if left unchecked.
Non-washable fabrics and upholstery Brush spores off (outdoors if possible), then spray with an anti-mildew solution to kill any which remain. Some items may need dry-cleaning. Take professional advice from a local museum if mildew has attacked any valuable textiles.
Washable fabrics Laundering is usually sufficient. On white fabrics (apart from nylon) mildew should be bleached with a 20-vol hydrogen peroxide solution (one part to six parts cold water). Household bleach is suitable for white cottons and linens which are not treated or have a specific finish. On coloured fabrics dampen the affected areas and rub with a block of hard household soap. Leave to dry in the sun or, in winter, by the sunniest window. Launder as usual.
Walls Wash with a mild detergent (for method see page 94), then paint over a solution of proprietary bactericide. It is always worth applying bactericide

before you redecorate a room with new wallcovering as this reduces the risk of mildew.

Plastic shower curtains Sponge with a weak solution of household bleach or antiseptic. This should clear light marking but bad marks should be treated with a detergent solution, then rinsed with proprietary bactericide.

Leather Sponge with a mild solution of household disinfectant (5ml to 500ml warm water). Wipe dry and buff with a soft cloth. Apply a thin layer of hide food (shoe polish on shoes).

Milk   Do not leave spilled milk to dry: the smell becomes virtually ineradicable. Squirt with a soda syphon or lukewarm water (not even hand-hot as this will set the stain) and blot thoroughly with kitchen paper.

Carpets Use a carpet shampoo followed by a stain remover if marks remain.

Non-washable fabrics and upholstery Sponge with lukewarm water then use a stain remover.

Washable fabrics Rinse in lukewarm water then soak in a biological detergent solution. Launder as appropriate.

Mud   Mud should always be allowed to dry so that you can brush off as much as possible with a stiff handbrush or vacuum cleaner tool before taking any further action.

Carpets Use a carpet shampoo followed by methylated spirit on any colour traces left by the mud.

Non-washable fabrics and upholstery Sponge with a warm solution of washing-up liquid, rinse with clear water and blot thoroughly.

Washable fabrics and clothing (not waterproofs) Brush dried mud off, use a stain remover on bad marks, then launder as usual.

Mustard   Powder and made-up mustards require the same treatment, although if you are having an item drycleaned you should tell the cleaner exactly what type of mustard it is – many contain extra flavourings which may affect treatment.

Washable fabrics Soak the stained area in a weak detergent solution, then sponge with a solution of ammonia (5ml to 500ml warm water). Launder as usual. Stains which have dried should be covered with a glycerine solution (equal parts glycerine and warm water) for an hour or so before rinsing and laundering.

Non-washable fabrics Dry-cleaning is the best treatment but you can sponge with a weak solution of detergent then dab remaining marks with an ammonia solution (5ml to 500ml warm water). Blot, then sponge with clear water. Do not apply this treatment to any fabric which will ringmark.

See tobacco and nicotine.

Nicotine

See also car, cycle, hair and paraffin oil.

Oil, fat and grease

Carpets Lay a pad of white blotting paper over the stain and apply a medium-hot iron to draw the grease into the paper. Take care not to damage any foam backing. Make up a strong solution of carpet shampoo and rub the lather into the marks. Wipe off with kitchen paper and repeat shampoo treatment until the marks disappear. Even when you think you have cleared a grease stain it may reappear days or weeks later as it works its way up the carpet pile. If it does, repeat the treatment.

Non-washable fabrics and upholstery Sprinkle on a layer of talcum powder or fuller's earth; as it absorbs the grease wipe or brush off and re-apply. Leave the final layer for several hours then brush off. Alternatively, use the blotting paper/iron treatment followed by a stain remover.

Washable fabrics Launder in the hottest water possible. On delicate fabrics and wool, dab with eucalyptus oil, then sponge or launder as appropriate.

Leather shoes, upholstery and handbags Oil can sometimes be wiped off before it sinks in. If it stains, cover the marks with a layer of bicycle puncture repair adhesive (having first checked on a test area that colour will not be affected). Leave it on for 24 hours, then peel off carefully. Apply shoe polish or hide food. Oil on a suede coat can sometimes be removed with the brush or block supplied. If this does not work have the garment cleaned professionally. For suede shoes blot with a face tissue, then rub with a block cleaner. If this fails rub a little lighter fuel on the stain with a ball of cotton wool. If colour is affected you will need to treat the whole of both shoes.

Paints Always treat while still fresh if possible. Dried paint is much harder to remove.
Acrylic Blot quickly with kitchen paper and wash in soapy water. Where a stain has dried put a pad of white cloth underneath it and dab with methylated spirit or a liquid grease solvent.
Oil paint Hold a pad of white cloth underneath and dab with white spirit, then sponge or launder. Hardened oil paint may respond to a liquid stain remover.
Poster, powder and water colours Sponge or soak in cold water. Launder garments, shampoo carpets and upholstery.
Emulsion and other water-based paint On carpets and upholstery, mop up and blot as much as possible, sponge with cold water and treat with a carpet/upholstery shampoo. Professional cleaning may be needed. If stains have dried soften them with methylated spirit (not acetates and triacetates) before treatment. On non-washable fabrics dried stains are best dry-cleaned.
Gloss and other oil-based paint Spoon up as much as possible and dab any residue with white spirit or a stain remover. Rinse with clean water and repeat.

Paraffin oil Blot quickly with kitchen paper.
Carpets Use an aerosol stain remover (call in professional cleaners if a large area is stained).
Non-washable and washable fabrics See oil, fat and grease.

Perspiration *Washable fabrics* Sponge with a solution of ammonia (5ml to 500ml warm water). Rinse immediately. Where colour has altered, sponge with a solution of white vinegar (15ml to 250ml warm water) and rinse before laundering. If appropriate for the fabric, soak in a biological detergent solution; otherwise launder as usual. Bleach marks out of white garments (other than nylon) with a solution of 20-vol hydrogen peroxide (one part to six parts cold water).

Non-washable fabrics Dab marks with a solution of white vinegar (15ml to 250ml warm water), which will also reduce any smell. Where colour has been affected, rub with methylated spirit (not acetates or triacetates – men's suits are frequently lined with these and should be cleaned professionally).

Plasticine and play-dough

Scrape up with a blunt knife. If possible put an absorbent pad under the stain and dab with a liquid stain remover to get rid of the deposit. Any remaining colour can be treated with methylated spirit. Launder washable fabrics, sponge non-washables and shampoo carpets and upholstery.

Rust

See iron mould.

Scent

Washable fabrics Rinse immediately. Cover dried stains with a glycerine solution (equal parts glycerine and warm water). Leave for an hour or more, then launder.

Non-washable fabrics Leave a glycerine solution on for an hour, then wipe over with a warm damp cloth and pat dry. Have expensive clothes cleaned professionally. Put perfume on *before* you dress.

Scorch marks

Carpets Beat with a stiff brush to remove loose pile. If a mark is not too bad the easiest solution may simply be to trim off the top of the pile using sharp embroidery scissors. Otherwise use a piece of coarse glasspaper and sand with a circular movement until the mark has become less obvious or disappeared. For bad scorch marks you may need to patch the area with an offcut, using a sharp knife and double-sided tape. Ensure that the pile of the offcut runs the same way as that of the rest of the carpet.

41

Non-washable fabrics Use a glycerine solution (equal parts glycerine and water) left on for an hour. Sponge off with warm water. A laundry borax solution (15ml to 500ml warm water) can fade bad marks: follow with clear water and repeat treatment if necessary.

Washable fabrics Rub marks with your fingers under cold running water, then soak the item in a laundry borax solution. Rinse and launder. Bad marks may never come out although on suitable white fabrics (not nylon) bleaching with a solution of 20-vol hydrogen peroxide (one part to six parts cold water) may do the trick.

Shoe polish Scrape up as much as possible.

Carpets, upholstery and non-washable fabrics Apply methylated spirit to marks, then use carpet or upholstery shampoo. A carpet spotting kit may prove useful.

Washable fabrics Use a stain remover or a few drops of ammonia in the rinse water when laundering. Treat bad marks with white spirit before washing.

Soot marks *Bricks* Brush well or use a vacuum cleaner attachment. Scrub marks using a hard scrubbing brush and clean water. If this fails, apply neat malt vinegar on a cloth or brush and then rinse thoroughly. Heavy staining should be treated with a solution of spirit of salts (one part to six parts cold water). Spirit of salts is corrosive, toxic and gives off poisonous fumes. Protect yourself suitably, open windows and ensure the solution does not come into contact with the pointing between the bricks. Rinse thoroughly with warm water.

Stonework Scrub with clear water, then use a mild solution of washing-up liquid on remaining marks. Bad stains may respond to an application of neat household bleach. Rinse well.

Spirits (alcoholic) *Carpets and upholstery* Blot up as much as possible and squirt the area with a soda syphon. If stains remain, use a carpet spotting kit or apply the lather of a carpet or upholstery shampoo. Dried-in spirit stains may respond to methylated spirit.

Non-washable fabrics Sponge with warm water and blot dry. Treat stains with a solution of washing-up liquid applied on a cloth. Wipe over with a clean wet cloth.

Washable fabrics Rinse in warm water and wash as usual.

Tar

Scrape up what you can, taking care not to damage carpet or fabric.

Carpets and non-washable fabrics Apply a glycerine solution (equal parts glycerine and water) to the marks and leave for an hour. Rinse with clear water. Use a carpet spotting kit or proprietary stain remover, then rinse with cold water.

Washable fabrics Put an absorbent white pad on top of the mark and apply eucalyptus oil on a cotton wool pad from below. Wash.

Shoes Use lighter fuel, checking first on an inconspicuous part that colour will not be affected.

Tea

Treat as soon as possible, particularly if it contains milk.

Carpets Mop up as much as possible and squirt with a soda syphon or clean with warm water. Use a carpet shampoo if the tea contained milk and then treat remaining stains with a stain remover. Dried marks should be sponged with a laundry borax solution (15ml to 500ml warm water) and rinsed. If marks remain, cover with a glycerine solution (equal parts glycerine and water), leave for an hour, then sponge off with clear water. Use a carpet shampoo.

Non-washable fabrics and upholstery Wipe over with a laundry borax solution (15ml laundry borax to 500ml warm water) followed by clear water. Pat well to remove moisture and when dry use an aerosol stain remover or upholstery spotting kit.

Washable fabrics Rinse in warm water and soak in a laundry borax solution (15ml to 500ml warm water) or biological detergent solution. Soften dried stains with a glycerine solution for an hour. Launder as usual.

Tablecloths should be rinsed under cold running water, then soaked in a biological detergent solution. Cloths with dry tea stains should be stretched over a bowl or basin and covered with laundry borax powder. Pour hot water through, then wash as usual. White fabrics can be cleaned with household bleach.

Tea spilled in bed on blankets should be rinsed out in warm water before laundering.

Tobacco and nicotine stains Apply neat sterilising fluid (for babies' bottles) on a pad of cotton wool to nicotine stains on the skin, then wash off.

Tomato ketchup and other bottled sauces Spoon and blot up as much as possible, taking care not to spread the stain.
Carpets Sponge with warm water and blot well. Apply lather from made-up carpet shampoo, wiping in the direction of the pile. Go over with a damp cloth. When dry use a stain remover on remaining marks.
Non-washable fabrics and upholstery Use a spoon or blunt knife to remove as much of the deposit as possible. Wipe over with a damp cloth, allow to dry and apply a proprietary stain remover. Tomato-based sauces are notoriously difficult to clear and may require professional treatment.
Washable fabrics Rinse the stained area in running cold water. Sponge with a soapflake solution and rinse well. Appropriate fabrics can be soaked in a biological detergent solution. Launder according to fabric.

Urine *Carpets* Squirt with a soda syphon and blot well with kitchen paper. Wipe over the area two or three times with cold water to which you have added a few drops of antiseptic. You can also buy a special carpet cleaner which contains deodorant. Remove dried urine stains by sponging with an ammonia solution (2.5ml to 500ml cold water).

Non-washable fabrics Sponge with cold water and blot well. Remove any stains with a solution of white vinegar (15ml to 500ml warm water). Dried stains will need professional attention.

Washable fabrics Rinse first in cold water, then launder as usual according to fabric. Old dried stains should be soaked in a biological detergent solution. Marks on appropriate white fabrics (not nylon) can be bleached with a solution of 20-vol hydrogen peroxide (one part to six parts cold water to which you have added a few drops of ammonia).

Mattresses Turn the mattress on its side to prevent water penetration. Hold a towel below the stain with one hand while you sponge the area with a cold solution of washing-up liquid or upholstery shampoo. Wipe over with clear water containing a few drops of antiseptic or sterilising fluid. Leave to dry thoroughly before returning to position. A mark will probably remain but the smell will have gone as will the urine chemicals which could otherwise rot the mattress's cover fabric.

Shoes Urine on leather shoes should be wiped off immediately with tissue paper and the area buffed up. For suede shoes rub marks with a cloth wrung out in clean warm water; while the shoes are still damp apply a suede brush to raise the nap. Dried marks may respond to a special shoe stain remover.

Scrape up as much deposit as possible.

Vomit

Carpets Flush with a soda syphon and blot well. Rub in the lather from a made-up solution of carpet shampoo; apply several times if necessary. Rinse with warm water to which you have added a few drops of antiseptic or use a carpet shampoo with a built-in deodorant.

Non-washable fabrics Clear as much as possible, then sponge the fabric with warm water containing a few drops of ammonia. Blot dry. Have delicate fabrics and expensive garments dry-cleaned professionally.

Washable fabrics Clear the deposit and rinse the fabric under cold running water. If suitable, soak and wash in a biological detergent solution; otherwise launder as usual.

Mattresses Turn the mattress on its side and, holding a towel below the stain with one hand, sponge the affected area with a warm solution of washing-up liquid or an upholstery shampoo. Wipe over with cold water containing a few drops of antiseptic. Blot well.

Water *Fabrics* Water marks are caused by the deposit of minerals from the water on to the fabric. Gentle scratching with a fingernail will sometimes remove them. Otherwise, hold the fabric in front of a steaming kettle spout for a few minutes, then, as it dries, rub the mark from the edge towards the centre. This treatment is not suitable for silk or chiffon.

Wine *Carpets* Fresh red wine stains will disappear when white wine is poured on them, but there are cheaper solutions: squirt a soda syphon on the stain and blot well. Apply the lather from made-up carpet shampoo two or three times, then wipe with a cloth wrung out in clean water. Blot well. Cover remaining traces with a glycerine solution (equal parts glycerine and water) and leave for an hour. Rinse with clear water and pat dry. Old red wine stains may come out with an application of methylated spirit. Sprinkling salt on to wine stains on carpets is an old wives' remedy; it creates a damp atmosphere that never dries out and always attracts dirt to the area. It is, however, a useful tip for preventing a wine stain from spreading over table linen.

Non-washable fabrics and upholstery Blot with kitchen paper, then sponge with warm water and blot again. Cover remaining stains with fuller's earth or talcum powder while still damp. Brush off after 10 minutes and apply another layer. Repeat applications until stain is lifted. Old dried stains should be covered with a glycerine solution (equal parts glycerine and water) left on for 30 minutes. Wipe over with clear water and if necessary use an upholstery spotting kit.

Washable fabrics Rinse in warm water and, if stains remain, soak in a laundry borax solution (15ml to 500ml warm water) or a biological detergent solution where suitable. Apply bleach to white fabrics with suitable finishes and use a solution of 20-vol hydrogen peroxide (one part to six parts cold water) on stained silk and wool.

3

GENERAL HOUSEHOLD CLEANING

The kitchen

The bathroom

Beds and bedding

Carpets and rugs

Curtains

Blinds

Upholstery

Floors

Walls and ceilings

Fireplaces

THE KITCHEN

Like the bathroom, the kitchen should be kept clean at all times. This is particularly difficult if your kitchen doubles as a laundry room; try not to sort your dirty washing on the worktops as this could be unhygienic. If your pets ever walk on the surfaces in the kitchen (this should not be encouraged), always prepare food on chopping boards.

Bakeware   As a general rule the less you wash bakeware the better it performs. Ideally, just wipe with kitchen paper after use.

Always follow any special care instructions; some non-stick bakeware, for example, should be washed in clear water only, without washing-up liquid.

Burnt deposits can be loosened by soaking in a boiling solution of washing soda; do not try to scrape deposits off non-stick items with a knife.

Bakeware made from tin should be dried immediately after washing to prevent rusting.

Bins   Kitchen bins should be emptied as soon as the contents start to smell, even if the bin liner is not full, and cleaned once a week with a solution of bleach or disinfectant (use the dilution strength recommended on the bottle). Always wear household gloves and protect your clothing from splashes. Drain the bin well after washing and if necessary wipe dry with kitchen paper. You will probably need to wash the bin top more often as they tend to attract dirt and splashes.

Always line kitchen bins before you put rubbish into them. Carrier bags are suitable for smaller bins; otherwise you will need to buy bin liners of the appropriate size. Some brands include a deodorising scent.

Bread bins   These should be washed out, rinsed and dried once a week. If mould develops, wash and wipe the interior with neat white vinegar. Allow to dry.

Chopping boards should be washed immediately after use.

Chopping boards

Wooden boards should be washed under hot running water and scrubbed with a washing-up brush if necessary. Wipe over the surface with a sterilising solution and stand the board on its long edge to dry naturally. Never soak a wooden board as this can cause warping. Where joints have opened up because of water seepage, lie the board flat and cover with a damp cloth for a few hours to make the wood swell. Wipe over with a little vegetable oil when dry. Always store the board on its side so that air can reach both surfaces. Smells can be removed by rubbing with half a lemon dipped in salt.

Plastic boards can usually be washed in the dishwasher. If not, wash as for wooden boards.

A wipe over with a damp cloth from time to time is usually sufficient for cooker exteriors. Clean off spills with washing-up liquid or household cleaner.

Cookers (see also microwave ovens, below)

Cooker hobs These should be wiped over when you finish cooking. Radiant and solid electric rings usually burn themselves clean. Solid hotplates may need cleaning with a cream cleaner or scouring pad; when clean they should be wiped over with a few drops of vegetable oil applied on kitchen paper to prevent rust developing.

Ceramic and halogen hobs should be cleaned with the product recommended by the manufacturer. Take care not to scratch the surface of glass-topped hobs as the scratch marks will be impossible to remove. Always use smooth-based saucepans and wipe the bases before putting them on the hob. Make sure that any cloth used for wiping the hob is free of grit. Wipe up any sticky spills immediately, otherwise the sugar in them will crystallise and cause pitting on the surface; for other spills, wait for the hob to cool.

Gas hobs Some parts of these may be removable. These should be cleaned from time to time by immersion in a hot solution of washing-up liquid, using a nylon cleaning pad to remove encrusted dirt. Alternatively, it may be possible to clean them in the dishwasher. Use a mild abrasive cleaner on stubborn stains. Mop up spills as soon as they occur, otherwise they will form a burnt deposit that is difficult to remove.

Cooker hoods The filter should be changed regularly and the hood washed thoroughly in a hot solution of washing-up liquid. Built-up grease can be removed with the back of a knife blade.

Grill pans These should be washed each time you use them, otherwise the build-up of dripped fat can become a fire hazard. Most grill pans can be washed in a dishwasher (check the handbook). Although this is a rather extravagant use of space, it is a lot easier and more effective than washing by hand. If you do not have a dishwasher, wash in a warm solution of washing-up liquid, using a stiff brush to get rid of any burnt-on soil.

Ovens These should be cleaned according to type. Untreated linings should be cleaned with a liquid or paste cleaner recommended by the Vitreous Enamel Development Council* applied on a nylon cleaning pad. Future soiling can be prevented by covering the floor and side panels of the oven with a thin paste of bicarbonate of soda and water. During cooking it dries and absorbs grease which can be wiped out easily afterwards – particularly helpful if you are roasting.

In theory, ovens with continuous clean linings clean themselves – provided you cook fairly often at a reasonably high temperature to ensure that fat is vaporised and not deposited. Wipe over with a damp cloth after cooking and always wipe up any spills on the floor of the oven.

PYROLYTIC CLEANING is a special process built in to some ovens. It requires you to set the empty oven to a very high temperature for a specified period of time. This turns the dirt to ashes which can be brushed out easily when the oven is cool.

Glass oven doors should always be cleaned when cool; the effect of a cold cleaner on warm glass can cause cracking. Light soiling can be tackled with a solution of washing-up liquid; for heavier dirt apply a paste or liquid cleaner on a nylon cleaning pad. Do not use an abrasive scourer or steel wool.

If you are cooking something in the oven which may bubble over – like a fruit pie – use a baking tray to catch the spills. It will be easier to clean than the floor of the oven.

Oven shelves can be cleaned in the dishwasher or soaked in a solution of biological detergent – or in the bath (protecting the bath surface with old towels) if your sink is not big enough.

Range cookers Food tends to carbonise on the hot plates and in the hot ovens, so it can be simply brushed off with a wire brush. Spills should be wiped out of the cooler ovens with a damp cloth as soon as you have finished cooking. If the spill is left it can be difficult to remove; if this is the case, use one of the cream cleaners approved by the Vitreous Enamel Development Council.*

To keep vitreous enamelled surfaces clean, wipe over regularly with a soapy damp cloth followed by a polish with a clean dry cloth. Mop up any spills containing acid (milk, fruit juice, etc.) immediately, as they can discolour the enamel.

Clean the insides of the hotplate lids and oven doors with a cream cleaner or a soap-impregnated pad, working in a circular motion. Do not immerse the oven doors in water as they contain insulation.

Cupboards Kitchen cupboards should be cleaned out regularly several times a year. Remove the food from each cupboard before starting and throw away any items which are past their best. Wash out the interior with a mild detergent solution, then rinse with warm water and dry with kitchen paper or an old towel. Leave for a couple of hours or longer before replacing the food, to ensure that any residual dampness has gone.

There is no need to line the bases of cupboards unless they are made of bare untreated wood, in which case use a proprietary lining paper or a roll of wallpaper. Do *not* use ready-pasted paper as bugs enjoy the flavour of the paste.

Dishwashers Wipe the exterior with a mild detergent solution and apply aerosol cleaner or polish. The interior should be cleaned from time to time when smells build up by running an empty cycle with a proprietary dishwasher cleaner. You can also buy perfumed sachets to hang from the top rack to overcome odours.

Extractor fans It is important that these are kept clean or they will not function properly. If you have them, follow the manufacturer's instructions for cleaning; if not, use the following method:
- Switch off at the mains.
- Remove the flex socket from the main part of the fan and unscrew the front-louvred grill.
- Clean the grill in a solution of washing-up liquid.
- Allow to drain, then wipe with kitchen paper or a clean cloth to ensure it is thoroughly dry.
- To clean the fan blades, either use an anti-static brush or unscrew the blade unit and wash in soapy water. Use a teapot brush to reach into any crannies in the motor and its support.
- Re-assemble all parts of the fan and give it a trial run to ensure it is working properly.

It is safest to wash the plastic parts by hand using a solution of washing-up liquid. Metal parts can usually be washed in a dishwasher, but check the instruction booklet. Keep the parts with electrical connections out of the water, and use a damp cloth to wipe over the surrounding areas.

Food processors

Defrosting Unless your freezer is of the frost-free variety, it will need defrosting when the ice has grown to a thickness of approximately 5mm. The more often you open the door, the more often you will need to defrost. The method is as follows:

Freezers

- Unplug the appliance.
- Put on gloves (special freezer gloves are available) to remove the frozen food and place it either in cool boxes or in the refrigerator. Cover with towels or blankets to increase insulation.
- Leave the freezer door open and place old towels on the freezer floor if it is a chest freezer or just in front of the freezer if it is an upright model.
- Place bowls of hot water on the shelves and in the bottom of the chest and keep renewing the water as it cools. (You can speed up drying with judicious use of a hair-dryer or fan-heater, but do not use the highest setting and do not put such appliances too near the freezer otherwise the seal may be damaged.)
- Use a wooden or plastic spatula to loosen and scrape off the ice as thawing gets under way. As towels become saturated, replace them with new ones.
- When defrosting is finished, dry the interior with a clean towel then rinse with a solution of bicarbonate of soda (15ml soda to 1 litre water)

Smells If smells linger, use a proprietary fridge/freezer cleaner or solution of sterilising fluid for babies' feeding bottles (one capful to 2 litres water) and allow to dry. Alternatively, fill the freezer with crumpled newspapers and leave it switched off with the door slightly ajar for a couple of days. The newspaper will absorb the smells. (You will need to call upon your neighbours to store your frozen food while this is going on.)

Stains These can be removed with neat bicarbonate of soda applied on a damp cloth.

To clean the freezer exterior, use a solution of washing-up liquid, then dry and spray with aerosol cleaner or polish.

Hostess trolleys Hostess trolleys are best cleaned while still warm (but not hot). A wipe-over with a damp cloth will usually remove any spills, but if fat or sugar has left burnt deposits apply a household cleaner suitable for worktops and floors. Do not use a scourer or a stiff brush as it may damage the surface.

Irons Always follow the manufacturer's instructions for cleaning both the inside and the base of your iron. Some steam irons need regular descaling, particularly in hard water areas. Use the descaling product recommended by the manufacturer.

Where scorching has occurred on the base, use very fine steel wool to remove the marks, taking care not to scratch the surface. Starch marks can be removed by rubbing the base of the iron with soap while still warm.

Kettles Kettles build up furry deposits, especially in hard water areas. Proprietary descaler products are available to treat this problem; always follow the instructions carefully. It is best to descale a kettle before the fur has formed a thick layer or you may have to repeat the treatment several times. Always wear protective gloves. The exterior should be wiped regularly.

Knives Wooden-handled knives must be washed by hand. Carbon steel-blade knives should be washed and dried immediately after use otherwise they will rust. They also tend to discolour when they come into contact with certain foods; stains can be removed with a nylon pad or abrasive cleaning powder.

Knife handles made from the same material as the blade are washable, but if the handle and blade are made separately and glued together with a tang (a sharp prong projecting from the blade) fixed in the handle, the knives are better washed by hand and dried immediately so that hot water cannot penetrate the join and loosen the adhesive.

Knife handles made from bone, ceramic, horn, ivory, mother-of-pearl and so on should be kept out of water and just polished with a soft cloth. You do not have to put them in your mouth so this is not unhygienic.

Microwave ovens

Wipe out the interior with a damp cloth if any spills occur. Keep the inside of the door and the seal scrupulously clean.

If smells build up, place a bowl of water containing 15ml lemon juice (bottled is fine) in the oven and run on high power for one minute. Remove the bowl and wipe round the oven cavity with a cloth, using the condensation which will have formed to clean it.

Plastics

Plastic items are generally safe in dishwashers if they are rigid; if flexible they are likely to melt and should be washed by hand. If stains build up on plastic tableware they can be removed with a very weak solution of bleach or denture cleaning powder.

Smelly plastic containers should be filled with a bicarbonate of soda solution (45ml to 500ml water) and left overnight before rinsing.

Refrigerators

Most modern refrigerators have an automatic defrosting device. If yours is an older model, switch off at the socket and defrost manually using the following method:
- Remove all food. Transfer perishable goods into a cool box containing freezer slabs.
- When defrosting is complete, remove the drip tray and empty out any water.

It is important not to damage the refrigerator while defrosting. The process can be speeded up by directing a hair-dryer or fan-heater on a low setting at the icy parts.

The fridge interior should be cleaned from time to time with a solution of bicarbonate of soda (15ml to 1 litre warm water), then dried well with a soft cloth. This is an odourless remedy unlike soap or detergent solutions and some proprietary fridge-cleaning products. Wash shelves and other fitments in a hot solution of washing-up liquid. Rinse and dry well before replacing.

If your fridge develops smells because of rotten food or because the power supply has been turned off, clear out all food and wash the interior several times with a bicarbonate of soda solution. Leave the fridge door open between washes until the smell has gone.

When you go away for any length of time (say, four weeks or more), empty the fridge of food and leave the door wedged slightly open so that air can circulate.

The exterior should be wiped over with a warm detergent solution. Dry and apply an aerosol cleaner/polish to keep dirt at bay.

Once or twice a year pull the fridge away from the wall and use your vacuum cleaner dusting attachment to remove dust from the grille on the back.

Roasting tins   Fill the tin with water and half a handful of washing soda. Boil for a few minutes, rinse and dry.

> **If you wash the roasting tin and replace it in the oven while the oven is still warm, the residual heat will dry it out.**

Saucepans   Saucepans come in a wide variety of materials and finishes, some of which require special care. If you buy a pan with an unusual finish, remember to keep the instructions; some of the more delicate finishes can be damaged by cleaning with the wrong product. Never put saucepans with wooden handles in the dishwasher unless the manufacturer states that the wood will be safe. Note too that some plastic handles may melt in the dishwasher, particularly if the pan is placed on the lower rack near the heating element.

To shift burnt-on deposits, fill the pan with a biological detergent solution and leave for a couple of hours, then bring it to the boil and remove as much deposit as possible. Severe stains may require several treatments.

Aluminium pans should be washed as soon as possible after use since food and water can cause the surface to pit. Wash either in the dishwasher or by hand and dry immediately. Use a scouring pad or steel wool soap pad to shine up the surface. If the interior has become discoloured, boil up a weak acid solution of apple peel or lemon juice in water. Rinse and dry. Do not use bleach.

Cast-iron pans should be washed immediately after use and dried at once, otherwise rust may develop. If it does, use a wire wool soap pad.

To remove food smells from any pan, boil a panful of water containing 30ml white vinegar. Switch on your extractor fan if you have one so that the smell of vinegar does not permeate the whole house.

Copper pans are usually lined with tin as the acids in certain foods react adversely with copper. Wash by hand, using a copper cleaner or salt and white vinegar to keep the exterior clean and shiny. Note that the lining of copper pans eventually wears thin and the pan will need to be recoated.

Non-stick pans should be cleaned according to the care instructions. Some are dishwasher-safe, others just need wiping out with kitchen paper. Note that even where the use of metal implements to remove burnt deposits is permitted, jabbing hard with them will damage the finish.

If washing non-stick ware by hand, take care not to use anything abrasive on the surface. A nylon pad should remove any grease deposits. If staining occurs, soak the pan in a solution of one cup of water, half a cup of household bleach and 30ml bicarbonate of soda. Boil this mixture for a few minutes, then wash, rinse and dry the pan.

Stainless steel pans can be washed by hand or in the dishwasher. Use a stainless steel cleaner to remove stains on the outside of the pan. The base may be aluminium or copper as these materials conduct heat better. Aluminium should be washed and copper cleaned with a copper cleaner. Do not soak stainless steel pans for long or pitting from mineral salts in the water may occur.

Vitreous enamel pans can be washed by hand or in the dishwasher. Stains on the outside of the pan should be removed with a product recommended by the Vitreous Enamel Development Council.* If the inside of the pan becomes stained, soak it in water with 5ml bleach for a few hours, then wash as normal.

A milk pan will be easier to clean if you rinse it out with cold water before heating the milk.

Sinks   When washing up in a sink, use a plastic bowl to protect the surface. Swill out the sink before putting in the bowl, as any trapped dirt or grit could scratch the surface of the sink.

Keep the plughole clean at all times, using a bottle brush. Pour a little bleach down the plughole once a week, taking care to avoid the surface of the sink. Leave for a couple of minutes, then rinse away.

Acrylic sinks These should be cared for with a cream cleaner; an application of white vinegar or lemon juice should remove stains.

Fireclay sinks and *vitreous enamel sinks* should be cleaned with a bath-cleaning product approved by the Vitreous Enamel Development Council.*

Stainless steel sinks These should be rinsed and dried at the end of each day to prevent water spotting. Remove grease and surface soiling with undiluted washing-up liquid. Never use abrasive cleaners or scouring pads. Polish with a proprietary sink cleaner or a stainless steel polish, rinse and dry.

BLOCKED SINKS

- Bale out as much water as possible, then pour down a solution of washing soda (one handful washing soda to a kettleful of boiling water). Be careful of splashes.
- If this does not work, stuff a rag into the overflow and place a sink plunger (available from hardware shops) over the plughole, having first greased the rim with petroleum jelly.
- Pump the plunger up and down a few times. This should build up enough pressure in the pipe to remove the blockage.

If you are still unsuccessful, put a bucket under the sink and unscrew the U-bend. Water will pour into the bucket and the blockage should be released at the same time. If not, use a straightened wire coat-hanger to poke around in the pipe and locate the blockage.

Tableware

Received wisdom about the order for washing-up by hand is glass, cutlery, then crockery, with a complete change of water between each lot. However, you can reverse the order if you prefer. Two sinks make the task easier; if you only have one, use a large plastic bowl for rinsing to speed up the process.

> Never wash very fine china, china with a hand-painted surface which is not safely glazed or china with a silver or gold trim in a dishwasher.

Cutlery (See also knives, above.) This should be washed as soon as possible after a meal, especially if made of silver or bronze (see page 118), which stain easily. Do not immerse bone or mother-of-pearl handles in water and *never* wash in a dishwasher.

Silver cutlery which is not used regularly should be wrapped in tarnish-proof cutlery rolls or paper. See silver, page 120.

> Do not wash silver and stainless steel cutlery together in a dishwasher: an electrolytic reaction could cause particles of silver to transfer on to the stainless steel.

Glasses and glassware Valuable glassware pieces should be washed individually and dried while still warm. Take care not to knock them on taps and wear household gloves which fit well to reduce the chance of dropping them. See drinking glasses, page 111.

Plates Whether using a dishwasher or washing by hand, first rinse off all food in warm water, or run the pre-wash program once you have stacked the plates in the machine. However, if the food residue is starchy or tenacious (mashed potato, egg, milk), rinse in cold water as warm water will make the residue more difficult to remove.

Greasy plates are easier to clean if first soaked in warm water with a little washing soda.

FISHY SMELLS

If fishy smells linger on plates, add a little vinegar to the final rinse water; cutlery should be rubbed with lemon juice and rinsed immediately.

Teapots

Teapots tend to build up tannin stains with use. Some people prefer not to wash them with detergent or in a dishwasher as they claim this taints the tea flavour. If you find this to be the case, be sure to rinse out the pot with water immediately after use.

China teapots Clean the inside by soaking in a solution of denture cleaner or a product designed to clean plastic tableware or picnicware. Rinse thoroughly after cleaning and leave off the lid so that any residual smell dissipates quickly.

Silver and stainless steel teapots Rinse after use and wash in a solution of washing-up liquid from time to time. The value of a silver teapot may be reduced if you use a strong chemical cleaner to get rid of tannin stains. Instead, rub with a handful of clean milk bottle tops or aluminium foil dipped in a solution of washing soda and boiling water. Leave for a few minutes, rinse and dry.

To prevent smells from building up in a silver or stainless steel teapot, leave three or four sugar lumps wrapped in muslin in the pot between uses. Make sure the teapot has been dried thoroughly before replacing the sugar lumps.

Toasters

These just need wiping over. The instructions should tell you how to remove crumbs from the inside. Never try to dislodge burnt particles with a sharp implement, even when the toaster is switched off at the socket.

Untreated wooden kitchen units
These will attract grease and dust, so wipe over regularly with a solution of washing-up liquid and apply a light coat of aerosol cleaner/polish. If dirt becomes a serious problem, clean the units thoroughly with a cream cleanser. Rinse, allow to dry and apply a coating of polyurethane seal. This will alter the appearance slightly but will make cleaning easier in future.

Vegetable racks
Line the bath with old towels to protect the bath's surface and fill with a solution of washing-up liquid. Use a scourer to get rid of ingrained dirt and rinse in clean water. Plastic and plastic-coated racks should be left to drain; metal racks should be dried immediately with an old towel.

Vacuum flasks
These should be washed out as soon as possible after use. If the smell of the liquid lingers, fill the flask with hot water and 15ml bicarbonate of soda. Store with the top off and a couple of sugar lumps inside to keep it fresh. Do not immerse in water as the flask will be damaged.

Waste disposal units
An electrical waste disposal unit is good for getting rid of food débris and is particularly useful if you live in an upstairs flat or anywhere that poses problems with disposing of rubbish.

Keep it clean, do not drop teaspoons down it and get rid of any smells by grinding up waste citrus peel from grapefruit, lemons and oranges.

Wooden items
Wood should be washed and dried immediately after use; do not soak, otherwise the wood may warp. Items which collect food débris such as chopping boards (see above), cheese and pastry boards and pastry rollers should be scraped gently first with a blunt knife.

Wooden salad bowls should be wiped out with kitchen paper or a cloth wrung out in clean warm water and left to dry naturally. They should not be washed. From time to time, season the outside of the bowl with a little vegetable oil and rub in well.

Worktops

Kitchen surfaces should be kept clean and dry at all times. Wash them after preparing food, using a cleaner containing bactericide, and dry with a kitchen towel.

Corian This should be washed and dried as recommended above. Marks can be removed with a household cleaner applied on an abrasive pad. Bad marks such as scorching can be sanded out with fine steel wool.

Laminated surfaces These are fairly tough but you should not chop food or put hot dishes down on them. Wash and dry as recommended above and remove stains with undiluted washing-up liquid or a non-abrasive household cleaner. Use abrasive creams only on very persistent stains. Smeary surfaces can be cleaned with a soft cloth dipped in white vinegar.

Textured-finish laminated surfaces These attract dirt and need frequent cleaning. Do not scrape at ingrained dirt but use a solution of washing-up liquid and a washing-up brush to remove it, scrubbing in a circular motion.

Tiled surfaces On heavily stained tiles use neat vinegar or a solution of household cleaner. Rinse and wipe dry. Watch out for food deposits which lodge in the grouting. Clean regularly with an old toothbrush dipped in a solution of household bleach.

THE BATHROOM

While you are unlikely to come to any harm if you do not clean the living and sleeping areas of your home very often, failure to clean the bathroom and kitchen could prove to be a health hazard. However daunting it may seem, it takes only a few minutes a day to keep the bathroom clean.

DAILY CLEANING

- Keep a bottle of washing-up liquid or bathroom cleaner and a cellulose sponge in the bathroom and encourage everyone to wipe round the bath and washbasin after use. This prevents hard water deposits and soap splashes building up.
- The lavatory should be checked daily and any dirt sticking to the bowl should be removed with a lavatory brush then flushed away. Once or twice a week, depending on the dirt level, clean more thoroughly.

Basins and bidets These are usually vitreous- or porcelain-enamelled and should be cleaned in the same way as baths (see below).

Baths These should be cleaned according to what they are made from. Keep and follow any manufacturers' instructions if you have a newly installed bath, or send off for a new set if you buy a home with a bath made from unfamiliar material.

Acrylic baths These should be rinsed and dried with a soft cloth after use, especially when bath cubes or bubble bath have been used, as these leave deposits on the surface. Clean with washing-up liquid. Where hard water deposits have built up, use a cream cleaner, rinse and buff. Where the surface is scratched, rub gently with a proprietary metal cleaner and buff well when the mark has gone.

Bear in mind that metal cleaner removes some of the top layer so try to avoid scratching the bath. Deep scratches can be eradicated by rubbing gently with very fine wet-and-dry paper (used wet). Rub with metal polish, rinse and buff.

Glass-fibre baths These need particular care as their colour is in the surface coating only; if rubbed with abrasives or metal polish the colour will eventually disappear. Clean regularly with washing-up liquid and avoid allowing deposits to build up or scratches to occur.

Vitrcous- and porcelain-enamelled baths These should be cleaned with one of the products recommended by the Vitreous Enamel Development Council.* Its symbol (see right) appears on approved products. Do not use harsh abrasives as they will eventually dull the bath's surface. Stubborn marks should respond to rubbing with paraffin, turpentine or white spirit. Rinse with a hot solution of washing-up liquid, then wipe dry.

Blue-green marks on enamel baths are the result of a constantly dripping tap. The washer should be changed and a vitreous enamel cleaner used, repeating several times if necessary.

BATHROOM MIRRORS AND WINDOWS

If you run cold water into the bath before hot, the bathroom windows and mirrors will not steam up so badly.
Rub bathroom mirrors with a little neat washing-up liquid to prevent condensation. (See glass, page 112.)

Tide marks should be treated with vitreous enamel cleaner. If the stain is very heavy, rub with white spirit, then rinse off immediately with a solution of washing-up liquid. Repeat if necessary until the mark clears but *do not* leave the white spirit to work on its own.

Use a proprietary bath stain remover for rust stains. Hard water marks should respond to a Vitreous Enamel Development Council-approved cleaner; otherwise use a sanitaryware cleaner that incorporates a scale remover.

Bath sealant which develops mouldy areas should be cleaned with household bleach applied on an old toothbrush. Take care not to get bleach on surrounding areas, towels or your clothes. Rinse thoroughly, then use a fungicidal wash to delay recurrence.

> **Do not leave your house plants in the bath whilst on holiday as chemicals from the soil can cause permanent staining.**

Ceramic tiles   Where soap splashes have built up, wipe over with a white vinegar solution (one part vinegar to four parts water), then rinse and wipe dry. Using a spray cleaner with a mould inhibitor is effective.

Dirty grouting should be cleaned with a bleach solution (one part bleach to six parts water) applied on an old toothbrush. Make sure the floor is protected from splashes. A proprietary grout cleaner can also be used.

Lavatories   Daily brushing and flushing and a once-a-week clean with a special lavatory cleaner should be sufficient for the lavatory bowl. Bleach is not generally recommended as it damages the ceramic glaze and makes the lavatory more difficult to clean; if you do use it, do not leave it for more than five minutes before flushing.

Where stains and hard water deposits have formed deep inside the bowl, you will first need to remove the water. The easiest way to do this is to bale it out using a disposable cup. Then apply thick, undiluted bleach to the stain and rinse off immediately; re-apply at intervals until the stain has gone. Hard water deposits should be covered with a thick paste of laundry borax and vinegar; leave for a couple of hours, then brush off and rinse. Ring marks can be removed with a proprietary limescale remover.

> Never mix different brands of lavatory cleaner, or lavatory cleaner and bleach, in the bowl at the same time. A chemical reaction may give off toxic fumes.

The *lavatory brush* should be washed regularly in hot soapy water and rinsed in cold water with a few drops of disinfectant to stiffen the bristles. Wash the holder as well, if you have one.

Wipe the *lavatory seat* on top and underneath once a day using a solution of warm water with a little disinfectant. Dry with kitchen paper. Keep a cloth specifically for this purpose and do not use it for anything else.

Wash the outside of the *lavatory pedestal* once a week.

Plugholes and overflows

Accumulated gunge should be cleaned out of these once a week, using a bottle brush or teapot spout brush. Pour down a little liquid bleach, leave for a couple of minutes then rinse with clear water; this will also help to eliminate smells.

Rubber bath and shower mats

These tend to collect dirt in their indentations and the only way to clean them is a good scrub with washing-up liquid and a brush. Rinse thoroughly so that slime does not develop, and clean the mats on a regular basis.

Rubber plugs

These should be cleaned with turpentine.

Showers

The *shower cubicle* should be wiped after use, including the curtain or doors. Leave the curtain slightly open so that air can circulate. If *shower curtains* develop mildew, first soak them in a bleach solution (one part to four parts water), then rinse and machine-wash. Hard water deposits on shower walls should be wiped over with neat white vinegar. Leave on for 15 minutes, then rinse with the shower-head. Slimy shower curtains should be soaked in warm water to which a little fabric conditioner has been added. Rinse and wipe dry.

A clogged *shower-head* should be taken apart and the pieces (apart from the rubber washer) soaked in neat white vinegar. Use an old toothbrush to remove sediment before putting the shower-head together again. Proprietary shower-head cleaners are also available.

Sponges and flannels If these become slimy, soak them in a white vinegar solution (15ml vinegar to 500ml water), then wash well.

Taps *Chromium taps* just need a wipe with a damp cloth. Buff dry. Greasy marks should come off with washing-up liquid; for more serious stains use a liquid metal cleaner or some metal-cleaning wadding – but nothing abrasive.

If the mouth of a tap is encrusted with limescale, fill a yoghurt pot with white vinegar or a proprietary limescale remover. Suspend the pot from the tap head with string so that the spout is immersed in the liquid. Check after an hour or so to see if the scale has gone and repeat if necessary. Wash and polish the tap.

Gold-plated taps need to be dried with a soft cloth after use, otherwise marks will appear. Do not use a proprietary cleaner as this will eventually wear away the surface.

CLEANING CHROME

To remove scale from the chrome areas of a bath or basin – the plughole, taps and soak-away – rub with half a lemon or with vinegar, then rinse off and dry with a paper towel.

BEDS AND BEDDING

Beds and bedding will last longer, and you will sleep better, if they are aired each day after use. The human body loses about 300ml of moisture a night and at least 20 minutes of thorough airing are needed for it to evaporate and dry out from a mattress and bedding. Encourage all members of your household to throw back their bedclothes when they get up, and always make beds *before* you start cleaning a room; otherwise, the dust that is produced will spoil the effect of your work.

Bed bases

These should be vacuumed, using the appropriate tool for the material – a soft dusting brush for upholstery, a crevice tool for wooden slats. Make sure that the castors run smoothly; use a little oil or aerosol lubricator if they seem stiff, taking care to protect the flooring.

Bedspreads (counterpanes)

These should be laundered or dry-cleaned according to the care label. Always air thoroughly after dry-cleaning to make sure that all the fumes have dissipated. (Specialist bedding cleaners should do this for you, but always check.) Do not use a coin-operated machine to clean bedding, because the fumes will linger within it unless you give it hours of outdoor airing.

Candlewick bedspreads should be dried on a clothes line with the fluffy side on the inside. To make the pile stand up, rub the insides together or tumble-dry. (Foam-backed candlewick *bath mats* should never be tumble-dryed.)

Blankets

Blankets may be made of natural or synthetic fibres or a mixture of the two. They benefit from a spell out of use so rotate your supply, storing those not in use in sealed plastic bags or special blanket bags (available from most department stores). Wash them before storing and put a moth-repellent sachet in with those containing any wool.

You can wash a blanket in a domestic washing-machine provided that it can hold it comfortably when dry. If the blanket is too big, wash by hand or take it to a launderette.

Follow the steps below when hand-washing a blanket.

- An initial soak in clean cold bath water will remove surface dirt, but if the blanket is heavily stained soak first in biological detergent, taking care to immerse the *entire* blanket in case of colour change.
- Wash in a solution of mild detergent (easier to rinse out than soapflakes), kneading with your hands so that all areas are agitated.
- Rinse several times in warm clear water, putting 30ml olive oil in the final rinse to soften the blanket.
- Empty the bath and wring out as much water as possible, pressing down hard with your hands. Do not twist the blanket (a tempting option when there are two people), as this can damage the fibres.
- Put the blanket in a spin-dryer if you have one, and tumble-dry if the care label permits. Otherwise let it dry naturally, preferably outdoors. (Note that the blanket will dry more quickly if you ensure that the two wet sides are not in contact with each other.)
- Always hang striped blankets with the colours running vertically so that colours stay in their intended lines.
- Air the blanket thoroughly before storing or use.

Electric blankets There are various kinds of electric blanket, from pre-heating underblankets which you switch on before you go to bed and then turn off, to low-voltage, all-night under- or overblankets. Electric duvets are also available. Always follow the manufacturer's care instructions for your own blanket. Many types can be washed but this should be done as infrequently as possible; fortunately regular washing is unlikely to be necessary.

Most manufacturers recommend that electric blankets are returned to them for servicing every two or three years, at which point they will advise you whether the blanket needs replacing and may offer a price reduction on a new model.

Do not fold electric blankets when storing them: this may damage the element. Ideally, leave them flat on a spare bed or between a mattress and a bed base.

Sheepskin and wool underblankets are washable. Use plenty of fabric conditioner when machine-washing; when hand-washing put a teaspoon of olive oil in the final rinse to keep the fabric soft and supple.

Duvets

Like pillows, duvets need regular and thorough airing, preferably in the open air. If this is not possible, drape the duvet over the bottom of a bedstead or a couple of chairbacks. A duvet cover should always be used to protect the duvet from body moisture and spills.

Treat spills on the duvet immediately by tying off the affected area tightly with string, having first shaken the filling away from the outer casing. Clean according to the stain and the fabric.

This method can also be used when you want to wash the whole duvet casing. Shake the filling down to one end and tie the string tightly round the middle. Wash half the duvet casing and allow to dry, then shake the filling to the other end and repeat the process.

Do not attempt to wash any duvet (even a single) in a domestic washing-machine. Duvets are so bulky when wet that they can damage the spin cycle. Go to a launderette or have the duvet cleaned professionally. For a list of cleaners in your area contact the Textile Services Association.*

PUTTING ON A CLEAN DUVET COVER

Putting on a clean duvet cover, especially a double or king-size one, can be tricky and tiring. It is easier with two people, but if you are alone turn the duvet cover inside-out and push your arms through the opening into the far corners. With one hand in each corner, grasp the two corresponding corners of the duvet through the cover and shake down vigorously so that the cover envelops the duvet; it will now be right-side-out.

Duvet covers, pillow cases and sheets

These should be washed according to the care label. Dark-dyed colours should be washed separately from other colours until you are sure that the item is colour-fast.

Mixed-fibre sheets etc. should not need ironing provided you fold them carefully as soon as they are dry.

Natural-fibre bedding looks better if it is ironed; this will be easier if you fold the item into four and attach it with three pegs to a clothes line. Iron when still slightly damp and air thoroughly before replacing on the bed.

After washing white cotton or linen sheets always place them at the bottom of the pile in the airing cupboard. Regular rotation and use prevents yellow marks developing on the folds.

Duvet covers, pillow cases and sheets will dry more quickly if pegged to form a 'bag'. To achieve this effect with a sheet, fold it once along its length and peg the two pairs of ends to the line. Peg a third of the way along one side and a third of the way along the other side. With duvet covers and pillow cases peg one side only so that a good-size opening is left for air to get into.

These should be dry-cleaned professionally and aired thoroughly before use to ensure no toxic fumes remain.

Eiderdowns

These are designed to be rolled up loosely each day so that air can circulate through them and the moisture dry out. Follow the manufacturer's instructions.

Futons

These stay in better condition for longer if a protective cover is put over the mattress casing. The cover should be washed at regular intervals according to the fabric.

Mattresses

Mattresses should be turned over as often as the manufacturer recommends (this is much easier if two people tackle the job) or, if no recommendation is given, monthly or more often when new and then at six-monthly intervals. Every three months the head and foot of the mattress should be reversed. *Foam mattresses* do not need to be turned but should still be reversed every three months. A *double mattress* should be turned more frequently if the two people who sleep on it are of very different weights.

Dust can be removed from a *sprung mattress* with a soft brush; if your vacuum cleaner has a soft-brush attachment, set it on a low suction level. It is important not to pull out the buttons or to disturb the filling. *Foam mattresses* should be vacuumed with a crevice tool attachment set on a low suction level.

Make sure that the bed is pulled out at least once a week and the floor underneath it vacuumed to collect any skin-scale or dust which has accumulated. (See pages 30 and 45 for information on getting stains out of mattresses.)

Pillows are either foam-filled or made from synthetic or natural fibres. Avoid natural fillings if you are asthmatic or allergic to feathers and down. Bear in mind that some foam tends to become lumpy with use.

Pillows

Pillows should be plumped up every day and both natural and synthetic-fibre pillows will benefit from an airing on a clothes line in fine, breezy weather.

As a general rule, pillows should be washed only when it is essential; even careful washing does not improve their texture. However, always read the care label as some are unaffected by washing. People with dust allergies should have their pillows cleaned regularly, either by hand-washing – in which case allow plenty of time for natural drying and airing – or in a machine. Bear in mind that a pillow becomes heavy when wet and may be too much for a small domestic machine; if this is the case, go to a launderette and use a centrifugal dryer to remove as much moisture as possible.

Never dry-clean pillows as it is impossible to ensure that all toxic fumes have been removed from the filling.

Hand-washing Pillows can be hand-washed in the bath using a solution of soapflakes or a mild detergent, using the following method:

- Knead the pillow quite vigorously in the suds so that all the filling is soaked.
- Rinse several times in clear warm water.
- Wring out as much water as possible by letting the water out of the bath and pressing down hard on the pillow.
- Roll the pillow in an old towel to stop it dripping on the floor.
- If you have a spin-dryer, spin the pillow for a maximum of 30 seconds (any longer and the filling could be damaged). Otherwise leave it to dry naturally, either pegged to a clothes line or spread on a special stretcher designed for drying jumpers flat. Do not tumble-dry.
- Air thoroughly before putting the pillow back on the bed.

Pillows will stay in better condition if you use two pillow cases. The double thickness prevents hair oil, face cream, etc. from seeping into the filling. Use an old pillow case for the inner layer.

For care of pillow cases, see page 74

> You can tell when a pillow is past its best by placing it horizontally over your forearm. If it holds its shape it's fine; if it droops badly at either end, you should invest in a new one.

See page 74. *Sheets*

CARPETS AND RUGS

New carpets should come supplied with care instructions. Keep these in a safe place and follow them carefully to ensure you get maximum wear out of the carpets. Some new carpets come with a protective coating such as Scotchgard. This can also be applied after fitting and should always be re-applied after shampooing.

Vacuuming

- The best way to keep carpets clean is to vacuum regularly – at least once a week and more often in areas where there is heavy wear.
- Always make sure your vacuum cleaner is set to the correct level of suction for the carpet you want to clean.
- Purists say you should go over each piece of carpet about eight times in order to be sure that it is thoroughly clean but most people are satisfied' with the results produced by a couple of forward and backward movements.
- Use any special attachments provided to reach under heavy pieces of furniture that cannot be moved and to clean around the edges of a room where dirt tends to accumulate.
- Some years ago it was received wisdom that you should not vacuum a new carpet until it had been laid down for several weeks. Manufacturers now encourage vacuuming as soon as a carpet is laid, and although you may find at first that it

sheds fluff at what appears to be an alarming rate, rest assured that removing the fluff does not harm the carpet.

● Some things, like dressmaking threads, pine needles and pet hairs, are difficult to vacuum up. Using an attachment may solve the problem, otherwise you may have to pick them off by hand. Pet hairs can be collected on a damp sponge.

Do not re-use vacuum cleaner bags unless the manufacturer says you can. With repeated use they become porous and do not trap the dust properly.

Long-pile (shag) carpets and *loop-pile carpets* should be cleaned with a suction-only vacuum cleaner; the rotating brush of an upright cleaner can abrade in long-pile or catch in loop-pile carpets. If you go over the pile before vacuuming with a carpet rake (available from carpet retailers, but do not use on loop-pile carpet) you will loosen any tangles and some embedded dirt. You should also rake the carpet after vacuuming if you want all the pile to lie in the same direction.

Where furniture has made a dent in a carpet, melt an ice-cube in the dent and raise the pile with a brush when dry.

Shampooing When a carpet becomes heavily soiled it will need to be shampooed. You can do this at home with a domestic or hired machine or call in a professional company to do it for you. (See page 80.)

In general *fitted carpets* are best cleaned in position since taking them up and sending them off to be cleaned may result in shrinkage. Extra costs for taking up and relaying the carpet may also be incurred.

Professional help It is best to seek professional help if you need to clean a large area of carpet, as it is a time-consuming and tiring job (however, see page 23). The National Carpet Cleaners' Association* will supply a list of its members. Professionals use machines which extract dirt from the bottom of the pile without over-wetting the carpet – important if the carpet is to keep its shape.

D-i-y If you are doing the job yourself, take care not to over-wet the carpet; this may distort the backing and cause colour from the backing to come through to the surface of the carpet.

Before shampooing, brush the carpet with a stiff brush to loosen embedded dirt, then vacuum thoroughly, going over each area several times.

Lightly soiled carpets can then be cleaned by using an absorbent cloth and a bucket of water. Do not use a detergent as it may leave a sticky residue which speeds up the rate of re-soiling; there is also a risk of colour change due to bleach and brighteners.

Heavily soiled carpets will need a full shampoo. If a carpet is fitted, check that it is firmly secured or it may become loose and lose its shape as you shampoo. Use a special carpet shampoo, following any recommendations made by the manufacturer of the machine you are using. Do not make the shampoo solution any stronger than is recommended, even if your carpet is filthy.

Work over the carpet in sections, blotting each section as you go with an old white towel, then brush the pile into the right direction with a clean carpet brush and allow to dry thoroughly. Repeat the whole process after a few days. (See Part 2, Stain Removal, for specific treatments.)

Nylon carpets create static and you may find you get slight shocks from metal items such as light switches and door fittings. If this becomes a problem, fill a plant spray container with water and 15ml fabric softener and spray on the carpet. Alternatively, you could call in a specialist firm to apply an anti-static coating.* This will need to be re-applied every time you shampoo the carpet.

Steam cleaning

Steam cleaning is an excellent method of getting dirt out of your carpets. A steam-cleaning machine works by injecting a blast of steam into the carpet and then sucking it back so that the dirt comes out with it. One great advantage is that the carpet does not become too wet. You can either hire a machine or call in a professional to do the job for you. It is worth noting that the machines are quite tiring to use; if you are not particularly fit or strong, professional help is recommended. (However, see page 23.)

Whether you clean your carpets yourself or employ a professional firm, you should ensure that small pieces of aluminium foil are put under any furniture legs which are in contact with the cleaned carpet (reliable firms will do this automatically). This is to prevent the furniture from staining the wet carpet. The foil should be left in position until the carpet is thoroughly dry (which may take a day or so). It is easier for whoever is cleaning the carpet if as much furniture as possible is removed from the room before cleaning starts.

Foam-backed carpets

Be careful when shampooing foam-backed carpets not to get the backing wet as water can distort the carpet. Either use a steam-cleaning machine or a dry shampoo. Foam-backed carpets should never be used where there is underfloor heating.

Oriental carpets should be treated with care; they are hand-made and the materials used may have different degrees of colour fastness. Vacuum with a cylinder cleaner (an upright will drag the fibres) and avoid the fringes, which can get sucked up into the appliance. Always vacuum in the direction in which the pile is intended to lie.

Oriental carpets

If a carpet is marked with grease, use a dry spot cleaner, testing first on an inconspicuous part of the carpet (perhaps the edge).

> **Test dye fastness by dampening a small area and seeing if loose dye comes off on to a white tissue. If it does, have the carpet cleaned by an expert.***

If applying any water-based treatment, sponge carefully and never allow water to penetrate to the back of the rug. Over-wetting of any kind can cause wool to distort.

Most rugs can be vacuumed and shampooed in the same way as carpets (see above). The manufacturer's label should give cleaning instructions.

Rugs

Do not shampoo *Chinese* or *Persian* rugs yourself but consult an expert (see oriental carpets, above).
Sheepskin rugs should be washed by hand using the following method:

- Boil together in a pan 1 litre water, 175g soapflakes and 50ml olive oil, stirring well so that the mixture emulsifies.
- Put the rug and mixture in a bath or large sink and add 50ml glycerine and enough warm water to cover the sheepskin.
- Wash well, making sure that all parts of the fleece are thoroughly agitated.

- Rinse once in deep warm water. Not all the soap will come out but some residue is important for retaining suppleness.
- Squeeze the rug to remove surplus water, then rub both sides of the sheepskin with a clean white towel.
- Hang the rug on a line in the open air until almost dry.
- Mix 125g fine oatmeal with 125g flour and rub the mixture into the underside of the rug; this replaces lost tanning materials and helps keep it soft.
- When the rug is completely dry, brush the wool to separate the strands.

Goatskin rugs should be cleaned professionally as goat hair is brittle and tends to break off if washed.

Rag rugs should be hand-washed in warm water with soapflakes.

Pull carefully into shape after washing and dry flat.

When vacuuming fringed rugs, use a vacuum cleaner attachment with an old stocking over the nozzle to prevent the fringe from being sucked up into the appliance.

CURTAINS

While in theory many curtain fabrics can be washed at home, you should remember that any lining or interlining may shrink at a different rate from the main fabric. Even the thread with which the curtains are sewn may shrink at a different rate and cause problems along the seams. If you have spent a lot of money on your curtains or a lot of time making them yourself it is probably better to have them cleaned professionally. Fancy finishes such as swags and tails should also be dry-cleaned.

Dust regularly using the soft brush attachment of your vacuum cleaner or a soft long-handled brush. Brushes with synthetic fibre bristles create static and are particularly good for collecting dust. It is also a good idea – provided you are sure you can rehang them correctly – to hang curtains outdoors on a dry breezy day.

Looking after curtains

- Follow the instructions supplied with the fabric.
- If you intend to machine-wash your curtains make sure that the dry weight fits comfortably in the drum; thick fabrics will become very heavy when wet.
- Measure the curtains before you wash them so that you can stretch them to the correct size afterwards. If you are worried about shrinkage, take down the hems before washing.
- Remove hooks and any weights and loosen the curtain tapes so that the curtains lie flat; if the curtain tapes are stitched in, dry-clean.
- Shake well to remove dust and run the soft brush attachment of the vacuum cleaner over each side. (Curtains will pick up less dust if this is done on a bed, not on the floor.)
- Soak curtains in a bathful of cold water to remove loose dirt, then either hand- or machine-wash according to the fabric instructions. In general, hand-washing is preferable since fabrics may be damaged by the harsher action of a machine.
- If hand-washing, do not rub or wring the fabric, just agitate it gently with your hands. Rinse thoroughly and either squeeze or spin-dry.
- Hang to dry over two parallel washing-lines. This may involve some improvisation with airers, chairbacks, etc. Make sure that the wet fabric does not touch any wood, which could stain it.
- While still just damp, iron the curtains on the wrong side, working along the vertical length. If some parts of the fabric have dried, dampen the whole curtain so that water marking does not occur.

Washing and drying curtains

- As you iron, stretch the seams gently to remove any puckering. When you have finished, spread out the curtain on a clean flat surface, perhaps a bed, and pull to the correct size.
- When the curtains are dry, insert hooks and weights and pull the tape to the correct width before rehanging.

> **Rehanging heavy curtains is best done by two people: one on a stepladder fixing the hooks, the other keeping the weight and bulk of the fabric off the ground.**

Net curtains   Net curtains should be washed on a regular basis *before* they start to look grubby. If dirt is visible, permanent discolouration may occur. Soak in cold water first to remove loose dirt, then wash. There is usually no need to iron, so rehang while still slightly damp and pull into shape.

> **Take advantage of curtains being down to clean the window embrasure thoroughly, including the inside of the glass and the windowsill. If polishing wooden windowsills, buff thoroughly so that no polish residue rubs off on to the hem of the curtain.**
>
> **Curtain cords should be kept dry, if possible, as they could shrink. Run a duster over them to remove loose dirt.**

Curtain rails   Clean while curtains are being washed. Stand on a steady stepladder and use the crevice tool attachment of a vacuum cleaner to remove dust from and behind the rail.

Brass and brass-effect curtain rails are lacquered and just need a thorough dusting.

Plastic rails should be washed in a solution of washing-up liquid, then rinsed in clear water. Either sponge the rails in position or take them down and clean in the bath. Gliders should be removed from the rail and soaked in a bowl of washing-up liquid solution, then rinsed. When tracks are clean and dry, spray the channel with an aerosol lubricant to ensure smooth running. Leave to dry before rehanging curtains.

Wooden rails should be dusted and given a light coating of polish. Rub in well so that no residue is absorbed by the curtain fabric.

Pelmets

Fabric If the pelmet is firmly fixed to the wall, brush regularly with the upholstery attachment of a vacuum cleaner. If it is dirty apply a little upholstery shampoo, taking care not to affect the shape. If the pelmet can be taken down, dry-clean or wash according to the fabric. Always use a dry-cleaner if the pelmet is lined, as the lining may shrink at a different rate from the main fabric. Give the dry-cleaner the pelmet measurements so that he can ensure it comes back the right size.

Wooden Dust with the crevice tool of your vacuum cleaner if you can reach, otherwise dust manually. Use a spray polish, and a cotton bud to get into any nooks where dirt has built up.

Plastic Wipe these over with a warm detergent solution, then rinse and buff dry.

Make sure all pelmets are dry before you re-hang, curtains.

BLINDS

Blinds should be cleaned according to their structure and fabric, as described in the instructions below.

As suggested on page 84, while cleaning blinds take the opportunity to give the window embrasure a thorough clean.

Bamboo   Use the upholstery attachment of a vacuum cleaner or a feather duster to remove dust from between the bamboo slats. Occasionally take the blind down, spread it out flat and wipe over with a cloth wrung out of a solution of washing-up liquid, Rinse with a clean damp cloth, taking care not to over-wet and distort the bamboo. Allow to dry naturally, away from direct heat.

Canvas   If possible, take down the blind and spread out on a clean surface outdoors (a patio or garden table covered with plastic sheeting). Scrub with a soft brush and detergent solution and rinse in cold water. Dry thoroughly before refixing. Canvas which is used outside can be treated with a water-proofing solution (available from camping shops).

Festoon (Austrian)   Vacuum frequently with a dusting attachment to prevent dirt settling in the folds. When the blind is dirty, take it down, loosen the vertical tapes until the blind is flat, then wash or dry-clean according to the fabric.

Pleated paper   Dust frequently to prevent dirt from building up in the creases. Use a little neat washing-up liquid to remove bad marks. Never immerse in water but wipe over with a damp cloth wrung out in clear warm water, taking care not to over-wet.

Roller   Dust regularly, using the soft brush attachment of the vacuum cleaner. Pay particular attention to the roller springs where a build-up of dust can cause malfunction. From time to time take the blind down, lie flat and vacuum each side. *Spongeable* fabric should be wiped over with a weak solution of washing-up liquid followed by a clean water rinse. Dry flat. You may wish to apply a coating of aerosol blind stiffener/protector. This is best done outdoors on a still day by pegging the blind to a clothes line. Remove marks from *non-spongeable* fabrics with an india rubber.

Dust regularly with a vacuum cleaner dusting attachment. Always dry-clean, as an exact right-angled finished shape is critical to their appearance.

Roman

Venetian blinds are difficult to dust conventionally. You can buy a special two- or three-pronged brush which cleans more than one slat at a time, or use the dusting attachment of a vacuum cleaner. Alternatively, buy a pair of soft cotton cleaning gloves and do the job with your hands. Wipe over the slats occasionally with a weak solution of house-hold detergent, then buff to a shine. (Wear protective gloves while doing this as the slats can cut your hands.) Wipe down the tapes with the same solution then with clear water. Leave to dry with the blinds hanging full-length so that the tapes do not shrink.

Venetian

If a kitchen blind has accumulated a build-up of grease, take it down and clean it in the bath, first laying down an old towel to protect the bath's surface. Wash in warm soapy water, then rinse, taking care to keep the roller mechanism dry. Hang up immediately, wipe down the tapes with a dry cloth and leave at full length until the tapes are dry. Venetian blinds will stay cleaner for longer if you apply a coating of anti-static polish.

UPHOLSTERY

Clean in position. If the fabric is expensive you may wish to call in a professional firm. Otherwise vacuum or brush the furniture, then use an upholstery shampoo, following the instructions supplied. Test first for colour change on an incon-spicuous part of the fabric. When the shampoo has dried thoroughly, vacuum or brush again to remove any shampoo residue and the dirt it has absorbed.

Fixed furniture covers

Leather covers should be cleaned by sponging with a damp cloth wiped over a tablet of glycerine soap. Do not over-wet. Wipe with a clean damp cloth but do not worry about getting out all the soap; it helps to keep the leather supple. Apply a thin coating of hide food from time to time and buff well so that it does not rub off on to clothes.

Plastic and vinyl should be wiped with warm soapy water, then with clean water, and buffed with a soft cloth. If the furniture has a wooden frame take care not to wet it as the colour may rub off on to the vinyl or plastic.

Loose covers Wash in the same way as curtains (see page 83). Most loose covers will be too bulky to fit into a domestic washing-machine and will have to be hand-washed.

Loose covers will shrink slightly as they dry and should be put back on furniture while still slightly damp so that they can be stretched into the correct position. Iron with the covers in position.

Glazed cotton covers can be hand-washed gently in warm water but do not wring or rub. Squeeze out moisture or spin-dry briefly and dry. Iron on the non-glazed side, using the cotton setting.

If cushions can be reversed, turn them once a week to stop them fading in sunlight.

Embroidered covers Embroidery should not be washed, treated with upholstery shampoo or any dry-cleaning product. Keep it free from dust by using a soft vacuum cleaner attachment on a low suction level. Fixed chair or stool seats with beading or raised threadwork of any kind are best brushed gently by hand with a baby's hairbrush.

Valuable embroidery should be cleaned professionally. The Royal School of Needlework* will do this or advise on a specialist firm in your area. If you need embroidery removed from chair or stool seats for cleaning, contact a professional upholsterer – or consult the Royal School of Needlework.

FLOORS

Ceramic tiles

These are easily cleaned with a mop or cloth dipped in a solution of washing-up liquid. Alternatively, clean with neat laundry borax applied on a damp mop or a solution of one part ammonia to three parts hot water. Polish with a chamois leather. A squeegee mop is best for this type of floor as it removes most of the water. Be careful when walking on wet ceramic tiles, particularly in rubber-soled shoes, as they are very slippery. Do not polish the tiles as this will make them permanently slippery.

Grouting between the tiles should be cleaned from time to time with an old toothbrush dipped into a strong solution of washing-up liquid or household cleaner. Alternatively, use a special grout cleaner.

Concrete

Concrete floors just need regular sweeping. To keep dust to a minimum apply two coats of a PVA adhesive and water mixture (one part adhesive to five parts water), allowing the first coat to dry before applying the second).

Cork tiles

These usually have a sealed, waxed or vinyl finish to prevent water and dirt from penetrating their porous surface. If you are laying cork tiles check that the edges as well as the surfaces are sealed or water may seep in from the sides.

Sealed cork just needs mopping over with warm water and an occasional application of emulsion polish.

Vinyl-finished cork should be damp-mopped with an occasional application of emulsion polish.

Waxed cork should be swept regularly with an occasional wax or liquid polish.

When applying any of these polishes try to avoid a build-up of polish around the edges of the room; this will eventually form a sticky deposit that attracts dirt and substances such as talcum powder in bathrooms. It looks very unattractive and is difficult to remove (use the back of a knife blade).

Always rinse floor mops in a disinfectant solution after use. Hang off the ground or upside-down to dry.

Linoleum

Linoleum is very tough but should never be over-wetted. Use a mop dampened in a weak solution of household cleaner, then apply a wax polish on living-room surfaces and an emulsion polish (which will not watermark) on kitchen and bathroom surfaces.

Natural floorcoverings

These include *cane, coconut matting, rush, sisal,* among other materials, and should be vacuumed regularly. When soiled, scrub first with salted and then clear water; these floorcoverings are damaged by detergents. Some specialist companies can supply natural flooring with a protective finish, applied before fitting, which keeps dirt at bay.*

Quarry tiles

Glazed tiles should be washed with a weak solution of household cleaner. They should be polished with a liquid or paste wax polish, preferably a non-slip product.

Unglazed tiles will need a more vigorous scrub with a stronger solution.

Always rinse with warm clear water and wipe over with a dry mop.

Faded tiles can be restored to their original colour. Remove the polish by rubbing with steel wool and white spirit, then wash with household cleaner, rinse and allow to dry. Apply a thin coat of coloured wax polish and rub it in well so that it doesn't come off on the soles of your shoes.

Newly-laid tiles tend to develop white patches, caused by lime working its way up through the concrete sub-floor. These can be removed temporarily by washing the tiles with a white vinegar solution (75ml vinegar to 5 litres water). Do not rinse off the solution and do not polish the tiles until the white patches cease to appear.

Rubber

Never use a synthetic detergent or solvent-based wax polish as rubber flooring is easily softened. Wash with a soapflake solution, rinse, dry and apply an emulsion polish.

If the floor is textured be careful not to let polish build up in the cracks.

Stone

Stone floors should be swept regularly and washed from time to time with a solution of washing soda (a handful to a bucket of warm water).

If your stone floor is in a kitchen or dining-room where greasy spills occur, it is a good idea to *seal* the stone in order to make cleaning easier and to prevent stains being absorbed. (See Addresses section for suppliers of sealant.) Before sealing ensure that the floor has been thoroughly cleaned; anything left on the surface will remain fixed under the sealant.

When cleaning floors of any material, do not use a cellulose mop with bleach solution, otherwise the mop will disintegrate.

Tiles

See ceramic tiles, cork tiles, quarry tiles.

Vinyl

Vinyl flooring will need less frequent washing if swept regularly. Mop with warm water (add a little household cleaner and rinse with clear water if the floor is dirty), and when the floor is dry apply an emulsion polish (a solvent-based wax polish will damage the surface).

When the emulsion polish starts to build up, remove it with the manufacturer's recommended product and start again from scratch.

Wood   Wood flooring with a *waxed surface* should be swept with a soft broom and dry-mopped to remove dust and loose soil. Sticky marks can be removed with a damp cloth wrung out in clean water. Waxed wood should *not* be washed as water can distort the wood. Apply a coating of wax polish paste with fine grain steel wool from time to time. When the polish builds up to an unacceptable level, i.e. when the floor starts to feel and look sticky, remove the old wax with a cloth dipped in white spirit. Allow to dry thoroughly before applying a new coating of wax.
Sealed wood floors should be damp-mopped to remove dust. Apply a coating of wax or emulsion polish from time to time for added shine.

TIP FOR ASTHMATICS

If you sprinkle damp tea leaves on to a dusty wooden floor before sweeping, this will prevent the dust from rising.

WALLS AND CEILINGS

Walls and ceilings should not be overlooked when you undertake a major clean of your home. Clear the room of as much clutter as possible and put dustsheets over any furniture that cannot be moved. Try to move items away from the walls so that you can work more quickly and efficiently.

Ceilings

Ceilings should not get very dirty unless there are smokers in the house or there is a coal fire in the room.

To clean high ceilings use a stepladder with wide steps, preferably a rail to hold on to, and a platform for your cleaning tools. Protective goggles and a nose and mouth mask are also a good idea.

Use either a long-handled ceiling brush or a vacuum cleaner dusting attachment. You can make your own ceiling brush by tying a clean duster over the head of a soft-bristled broom.

Do not bother to wash ceilings. A fresh coat of paint is more effective.

Grasscloth

This is difficult to clean as the grasses easily work loose. Use a soft brush vacuum cleaner attachment on low suction. Treat marks with an aerosol grease solvent. Avoid putting furniture against grasscloth as it rubs the grasses loose and leaves marks.

Hessian

Clean regularly with a vacuum cleaner attachment as its texture attracts dust. The dyes used in hessian wallcovering tend to run so do not wet or use stain-removal products. Treat marks with a chunk of crustless white bread.

Light fittings

To clean wall switches first make a template from thin card so that the cleaning product does not get on the wall. Then clean according to the material. For plastic switches use either an aerosol cleaner/polish or, if badly finger-marked, a little methylated spirit applied on a soft cloth. On metal fittings, use metal polish.

Clean plastic electrical sockets with methylated spirit, having switched off the electricity at the mains and taking care not to get any liquid in the holes.

DISCOLOURED WALLS ABOVE RADIATORS

Wallcoverings can be discoloured by dust rising in the hot air currents from radiators. To prevent this from happening, fit shelves above your radiators.

Painted walls   Dust and then wash with a warm solution of washing-up liquid. Do not use detergents which contain fluorescers as these can alter the colour of the paint.

If walls are very dirty, use either a weak solution of sugar soap or a diluted general-purpose household cleaner applied on a cellulose sponge or an absorbent cloth. Wash one section of the wall at a time – about one square metre – then rinse with clean water. Overlap the sections slightly to avoid tidemarks.

Wash walls from the bottom upwards as any dirty streaks which dribble down as you work are much easier to wipe off a clean surface than a dirty one. Clean really dirty patches with undiluted cleaning solution.

Do not stop when you have started to wash a wall, otherwise a tidemark will form between the clean and the dirty part which may be difficult to remove. If you are washing a wall which has light switches or electrical sockets, make sure the electricity supply is turned off and be careful not to get water in them.

Painted wood   Clean with an aerosol cleaner/polish. Badly soiled areas should be washed with a solution of washing-up liquid, then rinsed in clean water.

Skirting boards   *Painted skirting boards* should be washed with a solution of washing-up liquid, rinsed and dried. If

they are very dirty, wash first with sugar soap. Do not use household cleaners, which may affect the colour of the paint.
Unpainted wooden skirting boards should be dusted, then given a light coating of aerosol cleaner/polish.

Wash with a mild detergent solution and rinse with clean water. Take care not to over-wet the vinyl and avoid getting cleaning solution in the joins. Clean from the bottom upwards.

Vinyl wallcoverings

Wallpaper is easily damaged so work gently. Dust with a soft brush or the soft brush attachment of the vacuum cleaner. Take care not to flatten the pattern on textured wallpaper by pressing too hard.

Wallpaper

Do not wash wallpaper as the colours may run and the paper become detached from the wall. Clean soiled patches with a soft, clean india rubber or a chunk of crustless white bread.

Dust regularly with either a ceiling brush or a vacuum cleaner attachment.
Sealed panelling just needs wiping with a cloth wrung out in a mild detergent solution. Rinse with clean water and buff dry immediately. Maintain the shine with occasional use of an aerosol cleaner or polish.
Wax-finished panelling needs polishing with a good-quality wax paste once or twice a year. When the wax builds up and starts to smear and show fingerprints you should remove it with white spirit and re-apply. White spirit applied on fine steel wool and rubbed in the direction of the grain will also improve the appearance of faded and scratched panelling. Polish and buff.

Wood panelling

FIREPLACES

If you have a real fire in your home the fireplace is likely to become soiled with soot and smoke. If you let the dirt build up, it will be more difficult to clean than if you tackle it regularly.

Brick Brick fireplaces quickly become engrained with dirt, so brush the bricks regularly with a soft brush or vacuum cleaner attachment.

When dirt has built up, first try scrubbing with a hard brush and clean warm water. If this fails, scrub with neat white malt vinegar, then rinse. Do not use soap or detergent as they may be absorbed by the bricks and be very difficult to remove.

Heavy staining can be remedied with a solution of spirit of salts (one part to six parts water) but bear in mind that this is an extremely corrosive chemical and should not come into contact with your hands or clothes. Always wear protective goggles and make sure the room is well ventilated.

Cast iron *Rust build-up* can be removed with a wire brush or steel wool; make sure your eyes are protected. Take care not to damage any intricate decoration by brushing or rubbing too hard. Use a proprietary non-drip rust remover to get rid of any remaining residue, ensuring that you follow the manufacturer's instructions for application and neutralising.

To prevent further rust build-up, apply a thin layer of oil (vegetable oil is preferable as it has no smell).

Ceramic tiles Wash well with a solution of washing-up liquid. *Scorch marks* should come off with a non-abrasive household cleaner applied on a cloth (a brush can damage the glaze). Do not wipe the tiles when they are hot, otherwise the glaze may crack. Apply an aerosol cleaner/polish to prevent further soiling, then buff well.

Sponge with a weak solution of soapflakes, rinse and buff dry. If the fireplace has a polished finish, apply a marble polish* but avoid the areas which get hot.

Marble

If marble has become worn or chipped, special products to improve its appearance are available. (See Directory at back of book.)

Smooth Wipe over with a cloth wrung out well in washing-up liquid. Rinse with a cloth dipped sparingly in clean water and buff with a soft cloth. A marble polish (see above) will give it a good sheen but should not be used on areas affected by heat.

Slate

Riven If the rough surface attracts soot, scrub with a brush and a solution of washing-up liquid.

Sponge with clean warm water (the sponge will prevent soot from being absorbed into the stone). Where soiling is heavy, use a scrubbing brush and, if necessary, a solution of washing-up liquid. Do not use soap or scouring powder, which may alter the colour of the stone.

Stone

If you inherit a badly soiled stone fireplace, scrub it with a solution of bleach (one cup to a bucketful of water) but be sure to protect the floor, the surroundings and yourself.

4

CLEANING THE ARTICLES IN YOUR HOME

Around the house

Furniture

Glass

Jewellery

Metals

Ornamental materials

Leisure and hobby articles

Office equipment

AROUND THE HOUSE

There are fittings and ornaments in every household that are neglected when it comes to cleaning. Often it is just a matter of knowing what is the best method of cleaning to use, although some items are so commonplace, we simply forget to clean them. Valuable articles and mechanical objects are usually best left in the hands of an expert.

Basketware Use a brush or vacuum cleaner attachment (set at a low suction level) to remove dust. Wipe over with a damp cloth and allow to dry naturally.

Books Books are easily neglected as on the whole they do not show dirt. None the less, they do need care – even paperbacks. Take one book at a time and first blow, then dust, along the top with a soft cloth or feather duster while holding the book firmly closed to prevent dust slipping between the pages. Use an india rubber to remove surface dirt from any pages. Leather-bound books need special treatment to prevent their covers from cracking. Make up a soap solution by whisking a tablet of glycerine soap in warm water until a lather forms. Wipe over the leather with a barely damp cloth. Place the book on a clean white towel to dry naturally, then apply a thin coating of hide food. Valuable books should be checked regularly for any signs of deterioration and taken to a specialist bookseller or museum for advice or attention.

Bookshelves If you do not have time to clean bookshelves thoroughly, running the crevice tool of a vacuum cleaner along the front of the shelves not covered by books will remove a good amount of surface dust and should not damage most books (but do not do this if the books are very old or valuable).

Glass-fronted bookshelves are a good idea if you have a lot of books and not much time to clean; or ask a local leather supplier if you can get strips of leather to fix along the top edge of the shelves; this keeps dust from falling on to the tops of the books. An antiquarian book dealer should be able to put you in touch with a supplier. (See Addresses.) Use a polish suitable for the shelf surfaces, making sure that it is well rubbed in and will not come off on the books. If you find that books are infested with worm, first clean the shelves, then use an insecticidal spray. Finally, use a polish containing an anti-woodworm element.

Candlesticks

Chip off dried wax first. With silver and other suitable metal candlesticks, hold upside down and pour on boiling water to melt the remainder. On wooden and plastic candlesticks use a hair-dryer to melt the wax. Take care not to overheat the wood or it may crack.

Clocks

Clocks should be cleaned professionally. Dust and polish the exterior of longcase (grandfather) clocks but take care not to touch the weights inside. Do not clean the face. Wipe over any glass with methylated spirit; this also applies to the glass of carriage clocks. Old and valuable clocks should be covered with a plastic bag while you are dusting the room.

Flowers

Dried (and artificial) These can be cleaned with a hair-dryer on the lowest setting.
Silk Use either a feather duster or the cool setting of a hair dryer to remove dust from silk flowers. On no account wet them, otherwise the texture will be ruined. Clean them reasonably regularly to prevent dust building up to a level that is difficult to remove.

House plants

Dirty house plants will not thrive. Spray soft-leaved plants with clear water unless the instructions preclude this. Dust shiny-leaved plants with a soft cloth, then sponge with clean water or use a leaf-shining product very occasionally. Always use water at room temperature rather than cold.

Lampshades Keep free from dust so that as much light as possible can shine through. Dust regularly when you are cleaning a room and treat according to fabric when they become dirty.

Buckram lampshades may need brushing with a stiff brush if dust has become ingrained. Clean with a soft cloth dipped in turpentine, rubbing over the whole surface to avoid a patchy finish.

Parchment lampshades (the parchment is usually an imitation vegetable product) dissolve if wetted. Dust gently and remove marks with an india rubber.

Plastic lampshades may be fully washable, in which case clean in soapy water, rinse in clean water and dry thoroughly (otherwise the metal in the frame may rust). To avoid rusting, use a sponge instead of immersing the lampshade.

Vellum lampshades Shake together one part soapflakes, one part warm water and two parts methylated spirit in a screw-top jar. Wipe over the lampshade, then rinse with a cloth dipped in neat methylated spirit. Apply a thin coating of wax furniture polish, rubbed in carefully.

Pleated lampshades Remove dust by dabbing with double-width sticky tape.

Oil lamps The delicate glass chimneys are inclined to crack when washed. Use newspaper to wipe out the inside when it becomes coated with smoke. Soaking the wick in vinegar when it is new reduces smoking. Trim the wick off evenly after each use.

Papier mâché Dust regularly. Clean by wiping over occasionally with a cloth wrung out in soapy water, then wipe with clean water and immediately pat dry. Protect with a thin application of furniture cream.

Perspex Perspex scratches easily but light marks can be removed by rubbing over with a little metal polish in a circular movement. Clean with a solution of washing-up liquid, rinse off and dry. A light squirt from a spray cleaner/polish will help to maintain shine.

Pictures

Acrylic pictures Because acrylic paintings are not covered with glass they are particularly prone to discolouration by smoke from open fires and cigarettes. Do not attempt to clean them yourself but go to an expert (see Addresses).

For everyday care use a feather duster flicked gently over the surface unless the picture is valuable or has obviously loose flecks of paint, in which case leave well alone. In general hang acrylic pictures where they will not be affected by smoke.

Oil paintings Dust carefully using either a very soft cloth or a fluffy long-handled brush, taking care not to touch the canvas with the handle. Valuable oil paintings should be cleaned professionally. Alternatively, you can buy special picture-cleaner from art shops. If the painting is varnished, cleaning will remove this and you will need to have the picture re-varnished.

Prints and watercolours Have professionally treated if of monetary or sentimental value. Grease marks can be removed with an acetone solvent (available from art shops) applied on a soft cloth. Cover the mark with blotting paper and apply the tip of a warm iron to draw out the stain.

Picture frames

Gilded picture frames need frequent dusting. Use the soft attachment of a vacuum cleaner on intricately carved frames and cotton buds to reach into deep crevices. If discolouration occurs rub over the whole frame with a cloth dipped in turpentine substitute. You can touch up damaged spots with gilt wax (available from art shops) but the damage may still show. This treatment is not advisable for valuable frames. For gold leaf, see page 119.

Plastic picture frames should be wiped over with a damp cloth. Use neat washing-up liquid on any marks.

Wood frames should be dusted regularly. Polish occasionally with a little furniture cream, rubbed in well.

Radiators Use a vacuum cleaner tool to clean the front and top and as far behind as possible. Some fluffy brushes are narrow enough to use behind radiators; otherwise unwind a wire coat-hanger, make a loop at the end and tie a duster over it to do the job. Dirty painted radiators can be washed in a solution of heavy-duty household cleaner but check on a test patch first that this will not affect colour.

FURNITURE

Looking after furniture, even antique furniture, is less trouble than many people imagine. *Dusting* is the key to keeping it clean. *Polishing* needs to be done only infrequently and most modern furniture finishes just need a wipe-over from time to time.

It is important to know what your furniture is made from. Check and keep care labels when you buy new furniture and try to obtain as much information as possible about any older furniture you may acquire, particularly if it is valuable.

Antique Even though it has survived the ravages of time, antique furniture can easily be destroyed by central heating. Keep the room temperature at around 18°C/65°F and place a humidifier or bowl of water in the room. Don't place antiques near radiators.

On the whole, experts do not recommend polishes which contain silicones as they produce an unnatural finish. Use a good-quality non-silicone polish once or twice a year, buffing well to prevent a sticky build-up. Otherwise just dust and remove any greasy marks with a chamois leather wrung out in a vinegar solution (one part white vinegar to eight parts water). Antique furniture can also be cleaned professionally.*

**HOW TO MAKE YOUR OWN
SILICONE-FREE WAX POLISH**

You will need:
- **50g beeswax (available from craft and candle-making shops; the local library should also have a list of beekeepers)**
- **125ml turpentine (not turpentine substitute)**
Grate or chop the beeswax into a screw-top jar and add the turpentine. Stand the jar in a bowl of hot water until the wax melts. Screw on the lid and shake well. Use in very small quantities – a little goes a long way.

Bamboo

Dust with a vacuum cleaner attachment or a soft brush. If dirt is visible add 10ml laundry borax to a bowl of warm soapy water and clean with a scrubbing-brush. Rinse in warm salted water (10ml salt to 1 litre water) to stiffen and bleach it. Wipe dry, then apply a little furniture cream.

Cane

Remove dust with a brush or vacuum cleaner attachment. If unvarnished and dirty, rub with fine-gauge steel wool dampened in a solution of warm water and washing soda. Wipe over with cold water to rinse and stiffen it. Do not allow it to get very wet as this will soften it. *Varnished* cane just needs wiping over with a damp cloth.

French-polished wood

Remove sticky marks with a cloth wrung out well in warm soapy water. Where polish has built up (test by seeing if a finger leaves a print) remove with white spirit. Polish occasionally with good wax polish, otherwise just dust. If damaged by scratches or spills have the piece re-polished professionally.

Glass Use a window-cleaning product and buff well to remove smears. (See glass, page 112.)

Hides *Imitation hides* should be sponged with a lukewarm soapflake solution (never detergent), then rinsed with clear water and dried with a clean cloth. Buff with a soft duster.
Real hides (such as leather upholstery) should be dusted regularly. Dirt should be removed with a damp cloth which has been thoroughly wrung out in warm water and rubbed over a tablet of glycerine soap. Do not rinse, as leaving a little soap on the hide will help to keep it soft and supple. Apply a little hide food from time to time to help prevent cracking and stains. Rub in well so that it does not come off on clothes.

Leather desk-tops If ink is spilled, wipe it off immediately with tepid water on a clean soft cloth. For ballpoint ink use milk rather than water, then clean the whole leather area. If the surface is washable, use a damp cloth which has been rubbed over a tablet of glycerine soap. Leave to dry (the glycerine feeds the leather), then apply a thin coating of hide food. Apply hide food reasonably often to protect against stains.

Lloyd Loom Remove dust with a hair-dryer on its cool setting. Clean with a warm washing-up liquid solution, using a soft brush and taking care not to over-wet. Rinse with a cloth wrung out in warm water. Leave to dry naturally.

Oiled wood Never treat with traditional furniture polish; dust and apply a proprietary oil once or twice a year.

Ormolu See page 123.

Painted wood Check the finish to make sure that any cleaning other than dusting will not harm it. Check on an inconspicuous patch. If it can be cleaned, use a solution of washing-up liquid.

Pianos

Pianos with a polyester finish need a specialist product available from music shops.* French-polished pianos should be cleaned as described in the section on french-polished wood, above.

Ivory piano keys can be cleaned with a solution of methylated spirit and warm water (equal parts) applied on just-damp cotton wool balls. Badly discoloured keys need to be professionally scraped and re-polished. Otherwise just dust, then wipe over with a chamois leather wrung out in warm water containing a few drops of white vinegar. Do not let any liquid trickle down between the keys. Wipe dry.

Leaving the piano lid open on sunny days will stop keys from yellowing. Seek professional advice for valuable instruments.*

Plastic piano keys should be dusted regularly and cleaned with a chamois leather wrung out in warm water with a few drops of white vinegar added. Wipe dry. Plastic keys do not discolour.

Dust inside the case of the piano using the crevice tool attachment of a vacuum cleaner, avoiding the strings. For uprights, remove the bottom panel and vacuum away any fluff which has collected on the felt.

A piano should be kept in a room that is neither too dry nor too humid. Consult your piano-tuner for advice. Avoid fluctuations in temperature and keep heating below 22°C/ 72°F. Do not place a piano near windows, radiators or damp walls.

Plastic

An occasional wipe with a detergent solution followed by rinsing should be sufficient. Use an aerosol cleaner/polish to maintain shine and protect against dust.

Sealed wood

Dust regularly and wipe over with a damp cloth from time to time. A spray with cleaner or polish will maintain shine.

107

Teak   Teak should maintain a matt finish and be polished with a special teak cream or oil only once or twice a year. Rub well to ensure no sticky residue remains to attract dust. Dust regularly.

Upholstery   See page 87.

Waxed wood   Treat as antique furniture (see above).

Never mix different polishes on the same piece of furniture: a chemical reaction may occur.

FIRST AID FOR WOOD FURNITURE

Alcohol marks   Rub along the grain with cream metal polish.

Bruising and dents   Remove the finish with paint and varnish removers. Soak a piece of white blotting paper in water and fold to form a pad. Place over the mark and leave for 12 hours or overnight; cover with clingfilm so the pad does not dry out. This should make the wood grain swell. Remove the blotting paper and allow to dry naturally. Sand gently, following the grain. When smooth the surface should be finished with an appropriate varnishing product. This treatment is not suitable for french-polished wood and should not be used on valuable antiques.

A dent in *solid wood* may be raised by leaving a little warm water in the hollow. If this does not work, remove the wax finish with white spirit. Follow the instructions above for bruising, applying the tip of a warm iron to the blotting paper. When the wood has dried out use a wood colourstick or shoe polish to correct the colour.

A dent in *veneered wood* will need patching. Buy a small piece of matching veneer from a craft shop which stocks marquetry sets or from a furniture restorer. Trim it to a size that will cover the damaged area comfortably, making sure the grain runs the same way as the rest of the veneer. Place it over the dent and with a sharp craft knife cut an oval through both sections. Lift off the patch and remove the damaged veneer with a narrow wood chisel or a blunt knife. You may need to wet it to soften the glue. Clean any glue residue from the area.

Dampen the new veneer to make it flexible. Apply wood adhesive and press into position, wiping off any surplus adhesive. Smooth into position using the rounded handle of a screwdriver. Place a piece of brown paper over the repair and weigh it down. Leave to dry thoroughly, then smooth the edges of the patch with fine abrasive paper and use a wood colourstick or shoe polish to restore colour. Buff well.

Burns

Treat slight burns with cream metal polish, rubbing along the grain. Where a burn has roughened a solid wood surface, use a very sharp knife to scrape the surface, then sand with very fine abrasive paper and apply the wet blotting paper remedy described above under 'bruising'.

If the burn is deep, scrape with a sharp craft knife until the hole is clean. Use a matching shade of wood filler to fill the hole, smoothing it level with the surface. When dry, take a very fine artist's paintbrush and paint in the grain using artists' oil or watercolour paint of the right shade.

Cigarette burns Rub down with fine steel wool, then rub in a little linseed oil and leave overnight before polishing.

Heat marks

These appear white in colour. Rub in the direction of the grain with a cream metal polish.

Ink stains Use a cotton wool bud dipped in bleach, then dry quickly with kitchen paper. Re-apply as necessary. For large stains remove the wood finish, then use a proprietary wood bleach. Use a wood colourstick or shoe polish to restore colour before refinishing.

Scratches Use a wood colourstick, wax crayon or shoe polish.

Water marks Rub along the grain with cream metal polish. If the surface is rough, rub with very fine steel wool dipped in liquid wax polish.

GLASS

A smeary end-result is what most people want to avoid when cleaning glass. A perfect finish will depend very much upon the article being cleaned.

Carafes and decanters Try to rinse out immediately after use as these will stain if dregs are left in them for any length of time. The traditional method of cleaning is to roll lead shot around the base; an equally effective and simpler solution is to soak the inside in a warm solution of biological detergent or to mix up enough white vinegar and salt to cover the base. Leave either mixture for several hours, shaking at intervals. Rinse thoroughly with warm water until the smell of alcohol has disappeared and stand the glassware upside down to drain. Some ships' decanters have very wide bases and are not safe to turn upside down. If you use one regularly, invest in a fabric tube filled with moisture-absorbing crystals (see Addresses) or drain in a bucket padded with a towel.

Chandeliers Valuable glass chandeliers should be taken to pieces, cleaned and re-assembled by an expert unless you are *absolutely* confident of your ability to do it yourself. If you do decide to have a go, remember first to switch off at the mains the electricity on that circuit. Remove each piece of glass individually, wash it in a solution of washing-up liquid with a few drops of ammonia, rinse, drain on a non-fluffy cloth and polish with a chamois leather. You will need to be sure of how the various pieces fit together again; either follow the manufacturer's instructions or draw your own diagram.

To clean a chandelier without taking it down from the ceiling, use a step-ladder and rub over each piece with dry chamois leather gloves. Also available is chandelier aerosol* which you spray at the glass and allow to dry before polishing with a chamois leather or a soft cloth. If you use this method be sure to protect the floor below with plastic sheeting.

See Part 6, Outdoor Cleaning.

Conservatories and greenhouses

See carafes, above.

Decanters

Everyday drinking glasses can be washed by hand in warm washing-up liquid or in a dishwasher. Rinse, drain and polish with a soft, non-fluffy cloth. Always use fresh water and wash separately from crockery and cutlery. Use a plastic bowl to prevent them knocking against the hard surface of a sink and take care not to chip them on taps.

Drinking glasses

Cut glass and fine crystal should be washed by hand in warm washing-up liquid; repeated washing in a dishwasher will cause 'etching' – the build-up of white marking caused by strong detergent which is impossible to remove. Take care when drying stemmed glasses that you do not twist the stem too hard and break it away from the bowl.

> - Good-quality glasses should be stored upright as the rim is the easiest part to damage.
> - Do not stack cut-glass or crystal tumblers inside each other.

Furniture Items such as glass-fronted bookcases and cupboards and glass-topped tables should be cleaned with a proprietary window cleaner, or an aerosol cleaner or polish. Bad smears can be removed with methylated spirit applied on a cotton wool ball. Buff well, taking care that the cloth you use is completely free from grit.

Greenhouses See page 157.

Light bulbs Light bulbs will give off better light if cleaned every couple of months. Switch off the light and remove the bulb (wait until it is cool if necessary). Hold it at the fixing end and wipe over the glass with a barely damp cloth. Dry with a soft, non-fluffy cloth and replace. Fluorescent lighting tubes can be cleaned using the same method.

Mirrors Clean with a proprietary glass-cleaning product. In rooms such as bathrooms and kitchens where mirrors tend to mist over, use a product designed for car windscreens containing an anti-mist chemical (available from car accessory outlets). Never use water when cleaning a mirror. It can get between the glass and the silvering behind it and cause staining. This applies equally to modern bathroom cabinet mirrors and valuable antiques.

Oven doors See page 53.

Windows Always clean windows on dull days: sunlight dries them too quickly, producing smears. How often you clean the outside will very much depend on the area in which you live; the inside should be cleaned at least twice a year.

Many modern windows are of the 'tip and tilt' variety which makes them easy to clean both on the inside and on the outside and cuts out the need for using a ladder.

A proprietary window-cleaning product is best. Use sprays and aerosols for small areas and leaded lights. Alternatively, add either 100g laundry borax or 30ml vinegar to a small bucket of warm water and clean with a chamois leather. A 'wiper' blade is useful for tackling expanses of glass in clean sweeps and should be wiped after each stroke.

- Buff up clean dry glass with crumpled newspaper; the ink will add shine.
- Use an old toothbrush and a proprietary mould cleaner to get rid of black mould growing in window corners.

JEWELLERY

Both 'real' and costume jewellery need care in cleaning. Check valuable and antique jewellery first; if stones are loose or claws broken, get them repaired by a jeweller. It is a good idea to have any valuable items checked professionally once a year as a jeweller may detect weak spots that you haven't noticed. In addition, professional cleaning produces a shine that is hard to achieve at home. You could combine the cleaning with a revaluation of your jewellery for insurance purposes.

Do not use a chemical jewellery cleaner on costume jewellery unless you are sure that it will not discolour or lose its lacquer. Imitation gold and silver are best washed and dried.

Another option is to invest in a jewellery cleaning machine that works using sonic rays. These are fairly expensive so unless you own a large amount of jewellery and need to clean it on a regular basis it is more economical to use the methods described below.

CLEANING TIPS FOR JEWELLERY

- Use a plastic bowl filled with warm water and a little washing-up liquid. *Never* wash jewellery in a sink; if the plug becomes dislodged your jewellery may disappear down the drain.
- Place the jewellery in the washing solution, making sure that the items are not touching each other, and soak for a few minutes.
- Remove each piece individually and brush it gently with an old soft toothbrush (or a baby's toothbrush kept specifically for cleaning). If dirt or soap are difficult to get at, use a cocktail stick or toothpick to ease it out gently.
- Rinse the items well and place them on a clean linen tea-towel (not a fluffy one) to dry. Use the cool setting of a fan-heater or hair-dryer to speed up the process.
- Return the jewellery to its storage case, box or carrying roll. Do not leave pieces jumbled together in a drawer or they may become damaged. Diamonds, for example, can cut other stones and chains may become entangled. (If this happens, dust the chains lightly with talcum powder and use a sewing needle to disentangle them or remove the knots.)
- Before discarding the washing solution, drain it through a sieve to check that no stone, bead or earring has been overlooked.

Fragile stones

These include *amber*, *coral* and *jet*, and can be washed following the method described below. Never put fragile stones into a chemical solution. *Cameos* need special treatment and should not be washed or immersed in anything but cleaned with a soft brush dipped in a jewellery-cleaning solution.

Hard stones

These include *amethysts*, *diamonds*, *rubies* and *sapphires*, and can be cleaned using the treatment above or a chemical jewellery-cleaning solution. Another effective treatment is to soak them in a half-and-half solution of cold water and household ammonia, then drain on kitchen paper.

Emeralds

Emeralds are softer than other precious stones and chip easily. If you wash stones which are cracked, water will seep in and make any flaws visible. It is best to have emeralds cleaned professionally and to restrict home care to polishing with a clean, dry chamois leather.

Gold and platinum

These metal items may gather dirt for a long time before you actually notice it. Immerse them in methylated spirit for a couple of minutes, then rinse and dry well. Polish with a chamois leather.

Jade

Jade can be washed but should be dried immediately with a soft cloth or paper towel. Make sure that any cloth you use is free from grit as jade has a soft surface which scratches easily. A gentle wipe with a soft cloth should keep jade clean.

Marcasite

This should not be washed. Rub it over with a soft, dry toothbrush and polish with a chamois leather.

Opals and turquoise

These should never be washed. Rub them over with a chamois leather and use a soft toothbrush to clean any claw settings.

Pearls

These should never be washed as oils from the skin improve their sheen; the more you wear them the more they shine. If you wear them infrequently rub them gently with a chamois leather from time to time. Always apply hairspray, make-up or scent *before* putting on pearls, as these can damage their appearance.

Platinum See gold and platinum, above.

Silver Use a silver dip if you are in a hurry; no deposits from the dip will settle in the cracks. A better finish will be obtained with a silver polish, or by gently rubbing the item with a soft brush coated with toothpaste, then rinsing off. Solid silver items such as chunky bracelets are best cleaned with a long-term silver polish.

TIPS FOR KEEPING JEWELLERY IN GOOD ORDER

- Do not let set stones come into contact with household bleach while you are cleaning, as bleach may damage the metal mounts.
- Do not wear jewellery when you are doing any kind of rough work, such as d-i-y or gardening. A hard knock can damage even the toughest stone.
- Use a safety-pin to clip rings to your lapel or apron when you are cleaning or cooking.

METALS

Metals of one sort or another are found throughout the home, with a variety of uses from the functional to ornamental. An all-purpose metal cleaner is suitable for some, whilst others respond better to a specific cleaner.

See saucepans, page 59.

Aluminium

Brass should be cleaned with a proprietary metal polish. Using a 'long-term' variety will leave a film on the surface that reduces the build-up of tarnish. Slightly tarnished brass can be cleaned with a paste made from salt and lemon juice. Use a soft toothbrush to clean out any crevices.

Brass

Where there is a build-up of old metal polish on patterned brass, rub the affected area gently with very fine steel wool (gauge 0000), then wipe it over with a solution of 15g salt, 15ml white vinegar and 250ml hot (preferably distilled) water. Rinse immediately and wipe dry.

If verdigris (a green deposit) has developed, wipe over with ammonia, rinse and dry. Alternatively, soak in a warm solution of washing soda for several hours or use a proprietary verdigris remover.

Where brass is attached to other surfaces, e.g. a chest-of-drawers with brass handles, make a template of thin card and fix or hold it around the brass area so that it can be cleaned without coating the surrounding area with metal polish.

If brass is lacquered it is much easier to clean; you have only to wipe it over. To apply the lacquer, first make sure the brass is thoroughly clean and has the level of shine you like. Apply a transparent metal lacquer with either a soft brush (do two coats to make sure you do not miss any) or with a spray (in which case make sure the surrounding area is protected). From time to time you will need to remove the lacquer with a cellulose thinner and clean the brass before re-applying it.

Bronze is a sensitive metal that can be damaged by the chemicals in some cleaning fluids. Most bronze (except bronze cutlery) is intended to have a dull patina and will look unattractive if over-polished. Brush the surface regularly with a clean soft brush and use a cotton bud to clean out any crevices. If necessary, wash quickly with a solution of soapy water (stale beer is also recommended by some) and

Bronze

wipe dry. Apply a thin layer of dark brown shoe polish and buff with a chamois leather.

Cutlery is highly susceptible to staining from food and should be washed as soon as possible after meals, then dried and buffed with a soft cloth. Do not put it in a dishwasher as the detergent will be too strong. Clean once or twice a year with a general metal polish and wash and rinse thoroughly before use.

Marks on bronze can be removed with paraffin or turpentine applied on a soft cloth followed by a polish and buff. (See also cutlery, page 62.)

Outdoor ornaments are best left to build up a natural patina since it is impossible to keep them clean and shining.

Carbon steel See knives, page 56.

Cast iron See saucepans, page 59.

Chromium Chromium is a hard metal usually used as plating.

Bathroom fittings and taps should be dried after use. If limescale builds up, soak a cloth in malt vinegar and wrap around the affected areas. Where tap outlets are heavily limescaled, tie a yoghurt pot of vinegar to the tap, with the outlet in the vinegar, until the scale dissolves or can be chipped off easily.

Cars and bicycles Chromium should be washed, dried and protected with a heavy wax chrome cleaner at regular intervals.

Rust on chromium should be removed with wire wool or a proprietary rust remover. The surface should then be washed (using a neutralising solution if you have used a chemical rust remover), dried and sealed with a thin coat of polyurethane varnish. This will not look perfect but will prevent further rusting.

Chromium on furniture should be kept dusted and dry. Rub with a soft cloth to maintain shine and remove marks and smears with a little washing-up liquid or bicarbonate of soda applied on a damp cloth. Dry and buff.

Clean as for brass (see above).
Copper saucepans See page 59.

Copper

Enamel is found mainly on cookware (see saucepans, page 60); some ornamental household items are also enamelled. Wash in detergent and warm water and avoid abrasive cleaners and scourers as enamel scratches easily. Always use a plastic bowl in the sink otherwise heavy pots and pans may chip. See also baths, page 67.

Enamel

Gold does not tarnish so it needs only an occasional wash in warm soapy water, followed by rinsing and drying. Polish occasionally with a chamois leather to retain the shine. Tarnishing may occur if gold is part of an alloy; if this happens, immerse the item in a weak solution of ammonia.
Gold leaf, used particularly for picture frames, requires dusting only. If it becomes discoloured, dab it gently with a weak solution of ammonia. Gold-leaf paints can be used to touch up damaged areas but the paint will always stand out clearly from the original.

Gold

Pewter should keep its soft sheen and does not need to be polished in the same way as silver. If *antique* pewter is polished to a high shine it may well lose some of its value.

Pewter

Wash in soapy water, rinse, dry and buff to maintain a low sheen. Remove smears with methylated spirit on a cotton bud. Use a general metal polish if you want a shine.

Where pewter has corroded, rub with fine steel wool (gauge 0000) dipped in fine machine oil. Wipe dry and polish.

Never do anything other than wash and rinse the inside of pewter *tankards* or *goblets* as the metal absorbs smells permanently. Always rinse them immediately after use.

See jewellery, page 115.

Platinum

Silver and silver plate

There is a wide selection of silver cleaners on the market, formulated for different purposes. For silver and silver-plated cutlery that is used on a regular basis but tends to develop light or medium tarnish, use a silver dip which will remove it quickly so you can just rinse the cutlery under running water and polish it dry. The dips do not work well on heavy tarnishing (although repeated applications may clear it) and should not be used on silver-plated cutery with worn plating. For cutlery that is used only infrequently, use a polishing mitt or polishing gloves as necessary. For items which spend most of their time in storage use a silver polishing cloth that contains a tarnish inhibitor. If tarnishing is medium to heavy go for a silver paste which is applied on a damp sponge. This product foams up and is also good for removing tarnish from intricate sections where it can be difficult to polish. Cutlery needs to be kept dry to prevent tarnish. Do not wrap it in newspaper, brown paper, wool or rubber bands, all of which contain sulphur, which produces tarnish. You can buy special bags made from treated fabric for holding cutlery. Acid-free tissue paper also works well. If silver plating is damaged – and the item is not valuable – you can restore its shine with a silver-coating solution in which you immerse the item, or paint it on. It adds particles of silver to the surface and much improves the appearance. It is less suited to use on cutlery than on articles such as candlesticks and bowls.

Stainless steel

This is a tough metal, although it is stained easily by mineral salts in water so it should always be dried immediately after washing; a dishwasher will do this automatically. Do not soak stainless steel *cooking pans* for longer than necessary, otherwise pitting may develop. Polish occasionally with a proprietary product.

LACQUERED METALS

Lacquered metals need only a wipe-over with a damp cloth. However, if the lacquer becomes damaged you will need to remove it with an appropriate stripper and clean the metal thoroughly before re-applying the lacquer. Although lacquer prevents metals from discolouring, a coating will not last long and so is not worth applying to items which you touch a lot, such as door handles and light switches.

ORNAMENTAL MATERIALS

Alabaster

Alabaster is porous and should never be washed. Dip a chamois leather in a solution of washing-up liquid and wring out well. Treat stains with cotton wool dipped in turpentine, then buff with a dry chamois leather.

Do not put fresh flowers in an alabaster vase. The material is porous and the water will leach into it and eventually leak, ruining the appearance of the alabaster. Save the vase for dried, paper or silk flowers.

Bone

Bone should not be washed. Wipe over with methylated spirit on cotton wool. Polish any marks with a paste made from whiting (available from good art shops) and methylated spirit applied on a cotton bud. Bone which is very discoloured can be bleached with a paste made from 20-vol hydrogen peroxide and whiting; do not attempt this on anything valuable. See also knives, page 57.

Cloisonné Never use water or polish as it could get into the cracks and damage the enamel. Polish gently with an impregnated silver polishing cloth or simply dust carefully.

Ebony Never use water on ebony as this may damage it. Dust regularly, rubbing well when all dust is removed to retain shine. Very occasionally, apply a little furniture cream.

Ivory (see also pianos, page 107) The bleaching effect of sunlight is good for ivory but too much sunlight can cause cracking. Extreme cold can cause cracking too, so never leave, say, an ivory-backed hairbrush on a windowsill. Dust ivory regularly with a soft cloth using a clean, soft toothbrush to reach into any carved areas. Never place ivory in water as this can cause cracking. Wipe over pieces that are not particularly valuable (mirrors and hairbrushes) from time to time with methylated spirit applied on cotton wool.

Valuable antique ivory should be dusted regularly and cleaned professionally if it becomes severely discoloured.

When washing the bristles of an ivory hairbrush take care not to wet the ivory. Whisk the bristles in a warm soapflake solution, then in clear water. Tap the bristles on a clean white towel to remove as much water as possible and leave to dry naturally, bristles down and away from any heat source.

Avoid getting perfume or hairspray on ivory as they can cause discolouration.

Mother-of-pearl *Cutlery handles* See knives, page 57.
Inlays are usually found on tabletops and ornamental boxes. Clean the mother-of-pearl with a white furniture cream applied on a cloth or cotton bud. Take care not to touch other parts of the item if they are to be cleaned with another product. Otherwise use furniture cream over the whole surface.

Ornaments can be cleaned by making up a paste using powdered whiting (available from good art shops) and warm water. Apply with a soft cloth, then wash briefly in warm soapy water and rinse in warm water. Buff gently.

Onyx

Onyx is a porous substance which can even absorb sweat from hands. Hold it in a duster while you dust it with another. Remove light marks with cotton wool moistened in methylated spirit. Onyx table surfaces will absorb anything spilled on them, so wipe immediately. If liquid is absorbed, the onyx will need to be re-ground professionally to get rid of the mark and then re-polished.

Ormolu

Ormolu consists of gold leaf overlaid on bronze and is found on decorated furniture. Apply a solution of 10ml ammonia in a cup of warm water on a cotton bud, taking care not to spill any on surrounding wood. Make a cardboard template for larger areas. Rinse with clear water on a cotton wool ball and dry with a soft cloth. Do not use metal polish as this will damage the finish.

Soapstone

Soapstone is often used to make ornaments (particularly in Greece and Italy) and should be cleaned in the same way as bone (see above).

LEISURE AND HOBBY ITEMS

Binoculars and telescopes

Clean only on the outside. Consult a photographic dealer or other specialist if there is dirt inside. Wipe over the casing with a clean soft cloth after use. Clean the outside of lenses by dusting with a lint-free cloth, then with a cloth impregnated with a special lens-cleaning fluid (available from photographic dealers).

Cameras Unless you are an expert photographer and fully conversant with your photographic equipment it is best to leave its cleaning to an expert. Your local camera shop may be able to do it or put you in touch with someone who can.

Compact discs See records (below).

Embroidery See page 88.

Pianos See page 107.

Portable radios These tend to collect dust on plastic surfaces, particularly if used in the kitchen, where grease particles contribute to dirt build-up. Dust regularly with a feather or fluffy duster brush and from time to time use a cotton bud dipped in methylated spirit to clear grime from around knobs and dials.

Records and compact discs Use a specialist cleaning pack, available from record shops. Brush records (but not discs) before and after every use with a soft brush or velvet cleaning pad. Always put records back in their sleeves after use.

Sewing machines Clean the casing with a spray cleaner/polish, making sure that it is rubbed in well and will not get on to any fabric being sewn.

Use the brush supplied with the sewing machine (or buy one from a supplier) to brush out the residue of fabric 'lint' that collects underneath the bobbin.

Clean the machine every time you use it to prevent a build-up of lint.

Telescopes See binoculars (above).

Televisions and videos Clean the television cabinet with a product suitable for the material it is made from. If plastic, use an anti-static spray to prevent it attracting dust. Keep the screen clean by spraying window-cleaner over it once a week and buffing with a paper towel.

Cover your video recorder when it is not in use to prevent dust getting in the vents. Avoid standing drinks on top of it which, besides staining the top, could spill and damage the works. Do not use liquid cleaning products on your video recorder – just dust regularly. Silica gel sachets (from electrical retailers) should be put on top of the video recorder if the room is prone to condensation.

OFFICE EQUIPMENT

Many homes now boast at least one item of what was once regarded as 'office' equipment. But while items in an office are often maintained under service contracts, in your home they are your responsibility, and failure to keep them clean may result in expensive call-out charges for professional cleaning and repair.

When you buy a piece of equipment it should come with care instructions, perhaps even with specialised cleaning tools. Always follow the instructions carefully and try to clean the equipment once a week.

Answering machines

Dust with a synthetic fluffy brush. Apply a small amount of aerosol cleaner or polish on a soft clean cloth. Remove the tape(s) at intervals and dust the inside of the machine, either with a small battery-run vacuum cleaner or a damp cloth. Make sure the interior is dry before replacing the tapes.

Computers and word processors

Dust the *screen* before each use. Always use lint-free cloths or anti-static wipes. A little anti-static spray will help to keep dust at bay. Clean the outside of the machine by dusting and remove any marks with a damp cloth or methylated spirit. An aerosol cleaner or polish should be applied occasionally. The *keyboard* should be cleaned with methylated spirit applied on a cotton bud. Spray dusters are also available but are expensive.

Keep the screen and keyboard covered when not in use. When using the machine, keep tea, coffee etc. and cigarette ash at arm's length.

> **Always switch off electrical equipment before cleaning.**

Correction fluid spills
Allow the fluid to dry and with your nails or a blunt knife pick off as much as possible. On carpets and upholstery you may need to shampoo or call in a professional if the stain is bad. Once picked off, the fluid should wash out of clothes. Anything that needs dry-cleaning should be cleaned professionally — be sure to tell the cleaner what the mark is.

If correction fluid on a document gets on to the flatbed of a photocopier use methylated spirit to remove it. Never scrape the flatbed.

Fax machines
Dust with a small fluffy synthetic brush. If you rub the brush between your hands before use, it will create static which will pick up dust effectively. Use methylated spirit to clean off any marks and wipe the keypad with a cotton bud dipped in methylated spirit to keep the keys clean.

Photocopiers
See correction fluid spills, above.

Printers
Wipe over the exterior with a duster or anti-static cloth when dust builds up but leave the inside well alone. Provided you keep it closed, and possibly covered, dirt should not be a problem. Regular servicing will prevent the printer malfunctioning due to dust or grit inside it.

Telephones
Clean as for fax machines (above). If your telephone still has a dial, use a cotton bud dipped in methylated spirit to reach behind it. Wipe out the ear and mouthpieces with a little antiseptic fluid applied on cotton wool.

New typewriters usually come supplied with a
cleaning kit consisting of brushes and cleaning
fluid. Use the brush supplied or a small synthetic
fluffy brush to remove dust. Use methylated spirit
applied on a cotton bud to clean the keys and in
between them. Check the inside of the machine
once a week and use methylated spirit on a cotton
bud to remove any ink stains.

If you use your typewriter a lot, have it serviced
and cleaned professionally once a year. Keep covered when not in use.

Typewriters

See computers (above).

Wordprocessors

5

CARE OF CLOTHES, SHOES AND BAGS

Laundry

Dry-cleaning

Clothes

Sportswear

Shoes and bags

LAUNDRY

Getting good results from washing

Soaking If an item is very dirty, soak it first. Unless you have a large sink the bath is the best place. Make sure that the powder or liquid you use is fully dissolved *before* you soak the garment and that it is completely immersed. You may need to weigh down the garment with something like the bathrack.

If black clothes have faded it will usually be due to a build-up of soap. Unless the garment is dry-clean-only, soak in warm water with a little vinegar added to restore to former glory.

If you are using a biological powder check that it is suitable for use on the fabric. Soak for half an hour or so in lukewarm water or overnight in cold water. For a cold-water soak first dissolve the powder in a jug or bowl of hot water, then mix it into the cold water.

Use the specified amount of detergent for both machine- and hand-washing. If you use too little the garments will not be clean; using too much is wasteful.

Do not mix strong colours with white and pastel colours as the latter will eventually develop a greyish tinge and may pick up loose colour from the stronger dyes. If this happens, use a dye-removal product which takes out colour.

CHOOSING A WASHING POWDER

You will probably need more than one type of washing powder. The following should be sufficient for most people's needs:
- washing-machine powder or detergent suitable for coloured fabrics
- hand-washing powder or detergent containing bleach for white items
- biological soaking powder.

For dirty sports clothes or dirty work overalls you may need a heavier-duty product than would be necessary for averagely dirty washing.

Fabric conditioner This is used in addition to a washing product and reduces dirt-attracting static and creasing. However, after a time it can decrease the absorbency of towels. It makes ironing easier, particularly if you fold clothes carefully when they are dry. Fabric conditioner is available in two forms: as a liquid which goes in one of the detergent-dispensing drawers of the washing-machine and which is added to the last rinse, or as impregnated papers which are put into the tumble-dryer.

- Do not overload the washing-machine. The chart on page 136 shows how much items of clothing weigh. Make sure you do not overload the half-load program either.
- Try to mix large and small items in one load. If you just wash large items such as sheets, they tend to wrap around each other.

Before washing Check garments before you wash them. Do up zips and fastenings. Empty all pockets – coins can damage the machine, tissues will shred all over the wash-load, and bank notes will take time and effort to replace!

Wash delicate items which might snag inside a pillow case or purpose-made net bag.

Garments with a textured finish Always wash inside-out as the texture may be damaged by rubbing against other items.

Do not leave wet washing in the machine, where it may develop mildew. Tumble-dry or hang out somewhere airy. For the same reason, always wash and dry wet swimming costumes or rain-sodden clothes as soon as you can.

Hand-washing Hand-washing is recommended for items which cannot take the very hot water and high agitation levels of a washing-machine.

You may also prefer to hand-wash some items which are recommended for machine-washing, particularly if you think the colour might run.

CHECKING FOR COLOUR RUN

- Dampen a section of the item with water.
- Place a piece of white cotton rag or an old white handkerchief on top of the section and press down with an iron on the cool setting.
- If colour comes off on the handkerchief, the fabric is likely to run.
- Some colours run more than others. Red and deep-blue dyes are notorious.

Use soapflakes or a detergent specially formulated for hand-washing, making sure that the solution is completely dissolved before you put the clothes in. The best method is to dissolve the powder in a small bowl of hot water, then add this to the main wash water.

Although it is always sensible to wear household gloves when hand-washing, check the temperature of the water before you put them on – it is difficult to judge correctly with gloves on.

Soak dirty handkerchiefs overnight in salt water before washing, to loosen mucus.

Rinsing Do not skimp on rinsing. A washing-machine rinses several times and so must you. With some garments you can use the rinse and spin program of a washing-machine to remove water, although a spin-dryer is easier to control. If you have neither, squeeze the garment gently, placing delicate fabrics in a towel to absorb water.

Check whether items can be tumble-dried. If not, dry on a line or indoor airer. Sweaters should be pulled into shape and dried on a net frame (available from hardware shops) placed over the bath.

Understanding care labels

The chart on page 137 shows what the international care labels mean. If you are making up a mixed load for the washing-machine you should program it to wash at the lowest temperature given on a care label even if the other items can stand hotter water. However, to be really clean, fabrics need to be washed at the recommended temperature every third or fourth time round. The half-load facility which many machines have can be useful for this purpose.

Laundering household linen

Towels, bath mats, tablecloths and mats, napkins and tea-towels should all be laundered according to the instructions on the care label.

Rinse tea-towels in a weak starch solution after washing. This prevents them shedding fluff when drying china and glass.

Starching may sound old-fashioned but it does improve the appearance of cottons and linens and makes table linen look good for special occasions. Choose from traditional powder, instant powder or spray starch and follow the instructions. You can also buy a starching dip which is quick and easy to use. Remember to clean the iron (see page 56) after starching.

Laundering nappies

To prevent terry towelling nappies becoming heavily soiled, use disposable nappy liners inside them. These can be safely flushed down the lavatory.

Soak wet or soiled nappies in a proprietary nappy-soaking solution as soon as you take them off the baby, and leave the nappies in it until you are ready to wash them.

Take care to mix the solution according to the manufacturer's instructions. Nappies can be damaged if the solution is too strong as it contains a quantity of bleach.

Wash nappies at 95-100°C to clean and sterilise them. Keep an eye out for any irritation on the baby, such as a rash or soreness; some babies cannot tolerate biological washing powders.

Tumble-dry nappies and stack ready-folded to put on the baby.

STERILISING TEA-TOWELS

Ironing tea-towels has a sterilising effect – useful if you have laundered them at a low temperature in a mixed wash. Tea-towels can also be sterilised in a microwave oven. Put the towel on kitchen paper and microwave on high power for five minutes.

DETERGENT BUILD-UP ON TOWELS

Detergents can build up on towels, producing a whitish bloom on coloured fabrics. If this happens, machine-wash using the same amount of water-softening powder as you would detergent.

Cleaning washing-machines and tumble-dryers

The exterior should be wiped with a mild detergent solution followed by an application of aerosol cleaner/polish. Leave the washing-machine open for a while after removing a washload so that the interior can dry out and smells do not build up.

Remove the tumble-dryer filter after every session and clean off the fluff. Use a fluffy synthetic brush which becomes static when stroked or the crevice tool attachment of a vacuum cleaner. The hot air hose at the back should be cleaned regularly using the same method.

Washing-machines should be run on a clean-water-only cycle three or four times a year to clear any blockages.

Clean your washing-machine from time to time by running it with detergent but no load. In hard water areas add a little water softener to the detergent to get rid of any scale which has built up.

WASHING WEIGHTS FOR LAUNDRY

Garment	Fabric type	Weight
Denim jeans	cotton	700g (1lb 8oz)
Dress	cotton	500g (1lb 2oz)
	synthetic mix	350g (12 oz)
Man's shirt	cotton/synthetic mix	200g (7oz)
Nappies (10)	terry towelling	1000g (2lb 3oz)
Socks (1 pair)		50g (2oz)
T-shirt	cotton	100g (4oz)
Underwear (per item)		50g (2oz)
Woman's blouse/shirt	cotton	150g (5oz)
	synthetic mix	100g (4oz)
Household linens		
Bath towel		700g (1lb 8oz)
Duvet cover (double)	synthetic mix	1000g (2lb 3oz)
Duvet cover (single)	synthetic mix	700g (1lb 8oz)
Pillow case		150g (5oz)
Sheet (double)		500g (1lb 2oz)
Sheet (single)		450g (1lb)
Tablecloth (large)		700g (1lb 8oz)
Tablecloth (small)		250g (9oz)
Tea-towel		100g (4oz)

Note It is important not to overload your washing-machine, so use this list as a guide to making up a load. Clothes will get cleaner if they can move freely within the drum, so do not load the machine up to the maximum weight if it already appears full.

To weigh your own wash-load, put everything into a pillow case or a plastic carrier-bag. Either balance it on your bathroom scales or stand on them yourself, first with the bag and then without it. Subtract the difference.

CARE SYMBOLS

Words on label	Washing temperature	
	machine	**hand**
[95] wash in cotton cycle/ program *or* wash as cotton	very hot 95°C *normal action, rinse and spin*	hand hot 50°C
[60] wash in cotton cycle/ program *or* wash as cotton	hot 60°C	hand hot 50°C
[50] wash in synthetics cycle/ program *or* wash as synthetics	*reduced action, cold rinse, reduced spin or drip dry*	hand hot 50°C
[40] wash in cotton cycle/ program *or* wash as cotton	*normal action, rinse and spin*	warm 40°C
[40] wash in synthetics cycle/ program *or* wash as synthetics	*reduced action, cold rinse, reduced spin*	warm 40°C
[40] wash in wool cycle cycle/ program *or* wash as wool	*much reduced action, normal rinse*	warm 40°C
hand-wash	see garment label	
do not wash		

may be chlorine-bleached

do not chlorine-bleach

tumble-dry

do not tumble-dry

hot iron (cotton, linen, viscose)

warm iron (polyester mixtures, wool)

cool iron (acetate, acrylic, nylon, polyester, triacetate)

do not iron

Ⓐ dry-clean (in any solvents)

Ⓟ dry-clean (suitable for dry-cleaning with perchlorethylene, a chemical with high solvency power which is used in a particular type of machine. Seek the advice of a specialist dry-cleaning firm).

Ⓕ dry-clean in fluorocarbon. This chemical will be phased out by the end of 1994. Garments marked Ⓕ should be cleaned as in Ⓟ above. Good dry-cleaners will know how to moderate the solution to suit particular fabrics.

do not dry-clean

DRY-CLEANING

This is an essential cleaning process for items which cannot be washed. You may find that you buy a garment with a dry-clean-only label which you think you should be able to wash; this is a precaution used by some manufacturers who are concerned about dye running and shrinkage.

General care tips

If you do decide to wash an item which is labelled 'dry-clean only', wash separately by hand. This is not recommended for anything expensive or that you treasure but may save you money on, say, a dry-clean-only T-shirt which could cost several times its outlay in dry-cleaning.

Use a dry-cleaner who is a member of the British Laundry, Cleaning and Rental Services Ltd.* The organisation operates a code of practice and runs an arbitration service to help resolve disputes when things go wrong.

Note that dry-cleaning symbols sometimes specify a particular solvent (see chart on page 137); check that the dry-cleaner you intend to use has access to it. One dry-cleaning chemical called fluorocarbon is being phased out for environmental reasons. Garments marked with F should be cleaned in perchlorethylene: good dry-cleaners will know how to moderate the solution for the correct result on a particular fabric.

For very valuable or treasured items you may want to use a guaranteed high-quality cleaner who accepts items by post. Check what the cost will be in advance and also that items are insured while in transit.

Coin-operated dry-cleaning can be a bit hit and miss. If the outlet is completely unattended it is probably best to go elsewhere. The quality of the result will very much depend on how often the solvent in the machines is changed. Check this and try to be first in the queue when it has just been changed. Also check that the solvent used is suitable for what you are cleaning. Most coin-operated dry-cleaners use a basic chemical and you may find your care label specifies something else.

- tailored clothing which will lose its shape if washed
- jersey wool (unless labelled as washable)
- items with a special finish
- anything made of more than one fabric: washing may cause one fabric to shrink or lose colour at a different rate from the other.

Items which should be dry-cleaned

WAYS TO CUT YOUR DRY-CLEANING BILLS

- **Don't wear clothes two days running.**
- **Air clothes before putting them away.**
- **Brush outdoor clothes when you take them off and allow to dry naturally.**
- **Hang or fold clothes carefully after wearing.**
- **Treat stains as soon as they occur.**
- **Use an aerosol dry-cleaning product on grubby collars and cuffs.**

CLOTHES

Clothes repay care. If you look after them correctly they will continue to look good for longer. Fortunately, care labels are now stitched into every new garment.

General care tips
- When you take off your clothes at the end of the day you should check for any problems such as stains, loose threads and missing buttons.
- Remove any fluff or pilling which may have developed, either with a clothes-brush or by wrapping sticky tape round a finger and dabbing the affected area. Electrical devices to remove pilling are available but they tend to remove body from the fabric.
- Do not wear the same clothes two days running.
- If the clothes you have been wearing do not need washing, they will benefit from an airing before you put them away. Clothes tend to pick up smells – from outside sources as well as from your body. These will disperse more quickly in an open room than in a cupboard or chest-of-drawers.
- Brush garments (particularly coats and suits) when you take them off.
- Shiny patches on clothes can be remedied by mixing 10ml white vinegar in 250ml water and wiping with a cloth.

STORING CLOTHES

Clothes which are to be stored for some time – summer or winter garments, for example – should be cleaned first. Do not bother to iron things before you store them; you will only have to iron them again when you take them out. Avoid using fabric conditioner on clothes which are to be stored as this can accelerate mould growth.

Make sure that the place where you store clothes is dry and use a herbal or chemical moth-repellent.

WHITE SOCKS

Put 30ml bicarbonate of soda in the washing water and a squirt of lemon juice in the rinse water for really good results.

If your clothes are crushed and you do not have access to an iron, hang them in a steamy bathroom and the creases should drop out.

Some garments require special care if they are to maintain their shape and colour. Refer to the section below if you are in any doubt.

Hand- or machine-wash at a low temperature and do not wring. Iron while still damp. *Acetate*

Most acrylic garments can be machine-washed but always check the care label. Acrylic *jumpers* should be pulled into shape after washing and dried flat. *Acrylic*

Angora should be hand-washed in cool water. When dry use a teasel brush to raise the fluff. *Angora*

Wash or dry-clean according to the fabric. Iron gently so as not to flatten the brocade. *Velvet brocade* should be dry-cleaned by a specialist. *Brocade*

Wash or dry-clean according to the fabric. Iron gently, taking care not to enlarge the holes. If you are washing it together with items which have zips or hooks and eyes, enclose it in a pillow case. *Broderie anglaise*

Buckram   This should be dry-cleaned as washing makes it go floppy. It is important to check whether your curtain headings contain buckram: if they do they must be dry-cleaned, regardless of the fabric of the curtains themselves.

Canvas   Scrub with a stiff nailbrush and unperfumed soap. Rinse thoroughly.

Cashmere   Hand-wash in cool water. Use soapflakes or a specialist hand-washing product. Press inside-out with a cool iron.

Cheesecloth   Cheesecloth can be machine-washed and does not need ironing – simply pull into shape.

Chiffon   Chiffon should be hand-washed at a low temperature and ironed on a cool setting while damp. Valuable items should be dry-cleaned.

Corduroy   Wash inside-out according to care label. Iron inside-out while damp. Smooth the pile into the right direction with a soft cloth while drying.

Denim   Denim will shrink unless already pre-shrunk, as is the norm. Check the care label carefully. Wash separately until you are sure there is no colour run. Iron while very damp.

Jeans should be washed inside-out to avoid streaky lines on the denim.

Fur   Never store fur in plastic; always use a cotton or silk bag and hang on a well-padded hanger. Valuable furs will remain in better condition if put into cold storage during the warm months of the year.

Furs which are not worn regularly should be shaken from time to time.

Furs need to be dry-cleaned. If fur gets wet allow to dry naturally away from direct heat.

Lace

Valuable or antique lace should be given specialist care.* Otherwise, hand-wash in a mild detergent which does not contain bleach, which would rot it. If you have removed lace from a garment to wash it separately, make a template of the shape before washing so you can pull it back to the correct shape. Treat any stains before washing.

Dry flat on a white towel or jumper-drying rack; do not place in direct sunlight, which can cause it to yellow. Do not press unless essential, in which case cover the ironing-board with a white towel, put the lace face-downwards, cover with a cloth and press with a cool iron.

Leather and suede

Many leathers and suedes are genuinely washable, although some should only be sponged or dry-cleaned. Look carefully at the care label when you buy a leather garment. Leather or suede with a dull finish is easily stained, so use a spray protector at home or ask a dry-cleaner to do it for you. Always test first in an inconspicuous area to make sure there is no colour change.

To keep suede looking good you need to rub over it gently with a suede brush or another piece of suede.

Most leather and suede will need to be dry-cleaned occasionally. This always results in colour change, so make sure that you take all parts of a suit at the same time.

Linen

Test coloured linens for colour fastness (see page 132). Wash according to the care label. Iron while still quite damp.

Mohair

Wash as for angora (see above).

Muslin

Wash at high temperature. Stretch into shape while still damp.

Satin   Wash according to the care label. Dry-clean uphol-stery satin.

Seersucker   Wash according to the fibre and drip-dry. Do not iron, otherwise you will flatten the finish.

Silk   Most silk garments can now be machine-washed; otherwise hand-wash. Iron while slightly and evenly damp.

Suede   See leather and suede, above.

Velvet   Velvet can usually be machine- or hand-washed according to the care label. Dry-clean if you are con-cerned about colour run or damage.

CARING FOR CLOTHES

Dry-cleaning is expensive but with a little time and trouble you can cut down on the frequency.

- Carry a small clothes-brush or fluff-removing gadget with you. Often, all that is needed for a garment that is looking soiled is a good going-over to remove dust, débris, dandruff and so on.
- If you are away from home and a garment gets stained go for the soap and water treat-ment. Use the corner of a white towel and a little soap and water to attack whatever has been spilled.
- Consider carrying a small tube, stick or bot-tle of all-purpose grease solvent in your handbag, pocket or luggage.
- When you take off a garment do a quick spot-check to see if it needs attention. Collars and cuffs may benefit from a brush and sponge over with lukewarm water; muddy hems should be left to dry, brushed and sponged with warm water.
- Press garments which are not actually dirty but are beginning to look in need of a good clean.

(See Part 2, Stain Removal, for specific treatments.)

Viscose can be washed by hand or at low machine temperature. Stretch into shape while damp.

Viscose

Machine-wash on a delicates program. Use a cool iron while damp.

Viyella

These should be brushed well when dirty. Re-waterproofing products are available should you need them.*

Waterproofed fabrics

If the item is not machine-washable, wash by hand. When hand-washing woollens, it is sensible to draw the outline of the garment on a piece of white card or paper before washing. In this way you can stretch the item to its correct shape and size when drying. If you do not want line marks along the sleeves of jumpers, put an inner tube from clingfilm or kitchen foil into the sleeves, covering the tube with clingfilm first so that the cardboard does not mark the wool.

Wool

SPORTSWEAR

Grass stains tend to be the main problem. Dab with methylated spirit (not on acetates and triacetates) and rinse before laundering. If the flannels are dry-clean-only, cover the stain with an equal mixture of salt and cream of tartar and leave for 15 minutes. Brush off and repeat if the stain remains.

Cricket flannels

Brush to remove surface soil, then treat with a product designed to clean canvas shoes.

Cricket pads

If a cricket sweater starts to look grey, soak in a solution of proprietary water softener powder diluted according to the manufacturer's instructions.

Cricket sweaters

Riding macs Riding macs cannot normally be washed or dry-cleaned. In the absence of other instructions, scrub with a nailbrush dipped in a mild detergent solution, taking care to overlap on sections cleaned so that lines do not appear. Wipe over with a damp cloth, pat dry with a towel and hang to dry. Do not treat the inside.

Sailing gear Sailing gear should never be left lying around, otherwise it will develop mildew and permanent creases.
Guernseys should be hand-washed and rinsed, then placed in a pillow case and spun briefly. Dry over a clothes-line, turning frequently. Do not dry flat as the close knit means it will take a long time to dry and mildew may develop.
Heavy wool sweaters are best hand-washed. Soak in a cold hand-washing solution, then rinse in cold water. Do not rub or wring. Spin briefly in a washing-machine or spin-dryer, then dry flat.
Oiled-wool sweaters should be washed as infrequently as possible, as washing removes the oil. Use a warm soapflake solution and rinse in warm water containing 5ml olive oil. Dry flat.
Oilskins should not be washed or dry-cleaned but collars and cuffs can be rubbed with neat washing-up liquid, then sponged with clean water.

Swimming costumes Always rinse in cool clean water after swimming – whether in a pool or in the sea – and dry immediately. It is particularly important to remove chlorine and any suntan preparations.

Never leave a damp swimming costume in a plastic bag for more than a couple of hours as mildew will develop and the costume will rot.

If you swim a lot you should wash your costume regularly. Most are machine-washable, but you should never wring out, tumble-dry or place your costume on a radiator.

Trainers See page 148.

Whites White clothing such as tennis shorts and tops will need an occasional soak in biological detergent to brighten it up.

SHOES AND BAGS

Do not wear the same shoes two days running. When you take them off, leave them out to air for a while before putting them in a cupboard. Bags and luggage (pages 148–9) are worth keeping clean as dirt on these can easily rub off on clothes.

Fabric footwear

Fabrics vary from canvas to satin and should be treated accordingly. Slightly soiled fabrics can be cleaned with a proprietary shampoo suitable for the fabric. Wet the upper with a damp cloth, rub in the shampoo, then wipe over with a damp cloth. Brush when dry. Stuff shoes with newspaper or shoe trees when cleaning and dry at room temperature.

Colour can be restored with a whitener or coloured shoe-care product.

Some fabric shoes are machine-washable. If this is the case, wash the shoes with towels, otherwise they will make a lot of noise as they spin round the machine.

Gym shoes

See trainers, below.

Leather shoes

Patent leather Clean with a soft cloth and polish with an instant shoe-shine pad. When wet, stuff with newspaper and dry well away from any heat source, which could cause the leather to crack.

Smooth leather Remove any mud with a blunt piece of wood or the blunt edge of a knife, then sponge with a damp cloth. Stuff the shoes with newspaper or shoe trees to keep them in shape and allow to dry naturally away from any heat source. When dry, apply polish or shoe cream and allow to dry again, preferably overnight so that the polish can 'feed' the leather. Polish with a clean cloth or soft-bristled brush.

Suede Brush off dust regularly and remove mud with a nylon, rubber or soft brass wire suede-brush. Use a damp cloth to get rid of any residue. If the shoes are wet, allow them to dry naturally. Use a proprietary stain remover on oil and grease stains, applying several times if necessary. Check first on an inconspicuous area (e.g. the tongue of the shoe) that it will not leave a tide mark.

If the nap has been flattened, hold the shoe about 15cm from the spout of a steaming (not boiling) kettle, then brush using a circular motion. Use emery paper or a blunt knife to raise small areas of badly flattened nap.

If the colour has faded, use a proprietary dressing over the whole shoe, going over the paler areas first.

Riding boots Treat *leather* riding boots with good-quality leather food. Leave on overnight and buff the next day. Treat scratches with a coloured renovating polish. *Rubber* boots should just be rinsed under a cold tap.

Trainers Make sure gym or training shoes are completely dry before cleaning. Sponge off any dirt before whitening with a proprietary product. Most trainer manufacturers do not recommend machine-washing trainers, as it can weaken the support structures in the sole of the shoe. If you do wash trainers, ensure that any mud or dirt has been scraped off first.

Walking boots and shoes Treat with regular applications of leather food to keep them waterproof, and occasional applications of dubbin to keep them flexible.

Work boots Work boots should be cleaned immediately after wear as neglect will cause the leather to crack and the stitches to break. Remove mud, brush well and apply polish. From time to time, apply dubbin to keep the boots flexible. If you can afford two pairs and wear each of them only every other day they will last more than twice as long as shoes you wear day in, day out.

Bags *Fabric* These can be washed, either by hand or in a machine. Use a grease solvent to remove marks, then wipe over with a damp cloth and allow to dry away from direct heat. If the fabric is really dirty, and not too delicate, use a nailbrush and soapflake solution. Scrape or wipe off the soapy residue, then wipe over with a cloth and leave to dry naturally. It is a good idea to spray a new fabric bag with a protector before using it, to help repel dirt.

Lizard and other reptile skin This needs dusting very carefully in order not to loosen scales. An occasional application of hide food applied sparingly and rubbed in carefully will help to maintain its sheen.

Leather When removing from storage, and after use, brush well to remove dust and apply a thin coat of hide food. To clean, use a damp cloth rubbed over a glycerine soap tablet, then wipe with a warm damp cloth.

Straw/cane Use neat washing-up liquid on dirty or sticky marks, then wipe over with a damp cloth wrung out of cold water and leave to dry. Do not use warm water, which could cause the straw to distort. If the straw/cane is reasonably firm, you could apply an aerosol cleaner to help protect against dirt, but make sure it is thoroughly dry before using the bag.

Luggage

Hard luggage should be sponged over with a solution of washing-up liquid, rinsed and dried. A spray of cleaner/polish will help to protect the surface. Soft luggage may need an upholstery shampoo or a spray powder cleaner that brushes off.

Scratches on hard luggage are almost impossible to remove and must be borne like war scars. Damage to soft luggage usually needs a professional repair; take it to a luggage shop for a price estimate.

When storing luggage put a couple of sugar lumps in it. These will absorb musty smells until you need the cases again.

6

CLEANING OUTSIDE THE HOME

Outdoor cleaning

House exteriors

Gardens

Cars

Bicycles

OUTDOOR CLEANING

Keeping the exterior of your house clean is important, not only to maintain appearance but also to keep your property in good condition and functioning properly. The garden and all the things you use in it, such as tools, garden furniture and window boxes, need regular attention too. Cleaning cars and bicycles regularly allows you to keep an eye out for rust developing and small repairs that need doing.

HOUSE EXTERIORS

Make a positive resolution each spring to walk round the outside of your house and garden and note what needs doing. Use binoculars to check the roof and chimneypots – from the other side of the street or a neighbour's garden if necessary. Care of the exterior of flats is usually the responsibility of the landlord, an agent or an association of those who live in the block. Make sure that the exterior is checked annually.

Exterior walls   On the whole these do not need cleaning unless you live near the sea and find that salt has an adverse effect on a painted finish. You could wash exterior walls yourself but this is a laborious and tiring task and it is probably better to call in a professional firm with appropriate equipment or, in the case of painted walls, to have them repainted at regular intervals.

Exterior windows and conservatories   While you or your window-cleaner probably clean the glass on a regular basis, the frames also need attention. Wash them over with a solution of household cleaner, paying particular attention to the underside of sills where dirt can build up.

Check for gaps. Where the underside of the sill joins the wall is an area that is not instantly visible. Use a sealant to fill gaps and check wooden sills for rotting or splitting, which may mean replacing or repairing.

Check putty round the glass. Damaged areas should be chipped out and replaced before the putty falls out. Unless you have a good head for heights, upstairs windows are probably best repaired by a builder or glazier.

Airbricks prevent damp from entering the home at floor level and also offer under-floor ventilation. They should be kept clear and free of débris. If they are silted up, wash them with a detergent solution, using a small wire brush to clear the holes – a teapot spout brush is about the right size.

Airbricks

At the same time check that the damp-proof course has not been bridged by a build-up of soil. If it has, remove it so that the course is completely clear.

These should be inspected regularly; certainly more than once a year. Ground-level drain gullies should be cleared when débris builds up. Lift off the grid and use a trowel to scoop out what has collected. Pour neat household bleach down, making sure that as you pour you coat the sides of the gullies. This removes grease, kills germs and gets rid of smells. In hot weather when drains tend to become smelly you may need to do this frequently. Try to find a source of industrial-size containers of bleach – a local cleaning firm may be able to help.

Drains

Check manhole covers to see that they can be lifted easily. If they are cracked, replace them to prevent soil getting in. Clean the insides of a manhole with a solution of washing soda and hot water (one handful to a bucket). Use a long-handled, stiff-bristled brush.

Never plant new trees near drains; the roots can get into them and cause blocking. If existing trees (or a neighbour's tree roots) appear when you check drains take remedial action either by cutting the roots or having the trees removed altogether.

Many drain blockages are caused by unsuitable waste being put down the kitchen sink. To keep the pipes and drain clear put down neat household bleach or a solution of washing soda and hot water once a week.

Downpipes and gutters Gutters collect débris easily. Silt and soil form a breeding ground for weeds and grass which can block the gutters, causing water to run down the walls and cause dampness on the outside and inside of the house.

To check gutters, use a ladder but do not lean it against the gutter, which will not be strong enough to support it. Fit a ladder-stay which holds it slightly away from the wall.

Plug the downpipe with rags to prevent any débris you flush from the gutter getting into it and causing a blockage. If you are repainting the gutter protect the ground below from splashes with old sheets or plastic sheeting. (Do not stand the ladder on plastic sheeting or it may slip.)

Use a trowel to clear the débris from the gutter and save it for compost; the bird lime that will have inevitably accumulated makes it a good growing medium.

Plastic gutters can then be washed out using a solution of detergent. There is no need to rinse.

If you find, after you have sloshed your bucket of cleaning liquid through it, that water collects at any point in the gutter, it means that it is sagging and needs to have the brackets either tightened or renewed.

For metal gutters (now becoming rare), use a wire brush to scrape off any rust. Wash out and when dry touch up any bare metal with a rust inhibitor and apply a coat of zinc chromate primer, followed with a coat of bituminous paint.

If your gutters regularly become clogged up it could be worth fitting them with a wire gutter covering which prevents large pieces of débris from getting in. You will still have to check regularly for soil and weed growth.

Check that downpipes are not blocked at the top or at any point down the length by tipping a bucket of water down. If there is a blockage, dislodge it either with a length of strong wire, a bamboo cane or any long, strong tool you can improvise. You can buy wire coverings to shield drainpipes from blockages.

Consider painting downpipes with sticky anti-climb paint, which should deter burglars and will leave a distinctive mark on them if they touch it.

LADDER LORE

Before using any ladder, check its condition, especially if it is made of wood and has been stored outdoors. If rungs are loose or wood has split, get rid of it and either buy or hire a new one. You need a good ladder to carry out exterior checks and it is a false economy to use one that is not safe. When buying a new ladder consider whether a platform or tower would be more use (for example, for major exterior work such as repointing or repainting). A ladder with a stay that holds it away from the wall is useful, as is an attachment for holding a bucket or tools. Ladders also come with adjustable legs for use on uneven ground and with suction feet which prevent the ladder from moving on smooth ground.

Take care when setting up a ladder. You need a good firm base, so if you are working from soft earth get a solid board for the legs to rest on.

The distance from the foot of the ladder to the base of the wall should be about a quarter of the height of the ladder.

As a general rule, avoid doing ladder work in windy weather. In any case, tie the ladder to a firm support at the sides and base so that it will not slide sideways. This is particularly important with lightweigh' aluminium ladders.

Doormats For doormats made of coir, sisal and other tough natural materials nothing is better than a good beating, administered out of doors with a stiff brush. Stand clear of flying dust and débris or wear a protective mask. Always allow mud to dry before brushing it off. Stains are difficult to get out of stiff-pile doormats but it is always worth a try, using warm water and washing-up liquid applied on an old robust washing-up brush. Some doormats are washable, but after washing usually need to be sprayed with an aerosol dirt-repellent. These are the carpet-like mats found in many offices and office cleaning suppliers should be able to sell you replacement aerosols.

Dustbins Outdoor dustbins need not be cleaned as frequently as indoor bins. An outdoor tap and hose are probably the best options for cleaning a dustbin. Leave the bin to dry completely before you put in a new bin liner. Dustbins stay cleaner (and refuse collectors like you more) if you always use a dustbin liner for rubbish.

Clothes lines and rotary dryers Wipe along the line (where clothes will hang) before each use. Dried-on bird droppings may need treating with washing-up liquid. Lubricate the moving parts of a rotary dryer with light machine oil every few months. If rust develops, rub down to bare metal with wire wool and apply a suitable outdoor paint.

GARDENS

Paths, steps and patios The main problem with garden paths is weed growth, which is unsightly and can cause whatever the path is made from to break up.

Use either a spot weedkiller to deal with individual weeds or apply a path weedkiller, which should kill existing weeds and prevent re-growth for anything from several months to a year. Follow the instructions carefully regarding small children and pets. Wash out the container you use to apply it several times immediately after use.

Dirt and grime on paving and concrete can be removed with either a proprietary cleaner or a solution of household bleach (120ml to 5 litres cold water). This is just as effective as, and a lot cheaper than, proprietary patio cleaners. Use a stiff-bristled broom or a scrubbing brush to brush it over the surface, leave for a few minutes and rinse with clean water. Another option for cleaning patios is to hire a high-pressure water-sprayer. Wear goggles during use.

Where there is a build-up of algae (highly dangerous as it is slippery) use a liquid household cleaner containing bleach and make sure that every speck is removed. Do not use neat bleach to kill algae.

If after cleaning you find cracks, use an exterior filler applied on a trowel to repair them.

Drives

Clean concrete or paving stones in the same way as paths, steps and patios. Where there are oil stains use a proprietary paintbrush-cleaner followed by rinsing with a hose and clear water. Such treatment will not remove soaked-in oil on porous concrete, however: replacement, perhaps with an area of gravel which can itself be replaced as necessary, is the only real solution. Nor is the treatment suitable on asphalt, where sugar soap mixed according to the packet instructions should be used to shift stains.

Gates and fences

Repair or replace any sections which have become damaged. On wood use a stiff brush to clear attached débris, then apply an exterior wood preservative. For wrought iron, rub down any rust patches with steel wool and touch up with a rust inhibitor. If necessary, repaint with a suitable weatherproof product.

Greenhouses

If greenhouse glass is not clean, it will prevent the maximum amount of light getting in and plants will suffer. A clear-out once a year in the autumn will also prevent pests and diseases building up. Remove all plant débris, dead matter, leaves and rubbish first.

Scrub down the glass and frame, inside and out, plus any staging, using a solution of greenhouse disinfectant. Use a plastic plant label to remove dirt lodged in crevices around the edges of the glass.

When cleaning the roof glass you may find it easier to use a soft broom. Clean and sterilise pots and put old compost to use elsewhere in the garden.

An alternative way to rid the greenhouse of pests is to fumigate it. To do this check the cubic capacity (measure height x width x length) and purchase the appropriate quantity of fumigation pellets or a canister. Use masking tape to block any gaps in the greenhouse, then follow the instructions for fumigation.

Sheds Choose a fine day to clear out your shed. Use the opportunity to get rid of things you do not use and products that have lost their labels or are past their use-by date.

When it is empty, use a long-handled brush to dust the roof and walls, giving any spiders the chance to run for their lives, and then sweep the floor.

If your shed is in an extremely dank part of the garden, or the wood is in permanent contact with moist soil, you may need to rub down the outside of the shed with fine steel wool and apply a coat of preservative annually.

Check the roofing felt and secure any area which has come loose. Replace the felt if it becomes damaged.

Garden furniture Whether you keep it indoors or out, garden furniture needs care according to what it is made from.
Tubular metal After the winter, carefully open folding chairs and loungers. If the hinges are stiff, use an aerosol lubricant, otherwise apply a drop of light oil, taking care not to get it on any fabric.

Wipe over the frame with a damp cloth wrung out of washing-up liquid solution, then apply a little wax polish to give a shine.

Covers are usually rot-proof canvas or plastic and just need wiping over with a damp cloth. Mend any tears with a patch or strong thread and replace any covers which are too worn to be safe.

Cast iron and steel Oil hinges and treat any rust patches or chips with a proprietary rust remover. Then paint with a metal primer followed by exterior-quality gloss paint.

An enamelled finish just needs wiping or hosing over with clear water.

Wood Remove dust with a soft cloth, then use fine steel wool or glasspaper to smooth the surface. Dust again, then apply a lacquer seal or exterior-quality varnish, which will last for years unless the furniture legs are in contact with moist soil throughout the winter.

Hardwood will withstand all weathers but will change colour unless sealed. If you have sealed it yourself or bought sealed hardwood you will need to rub it down each autumn and apply a fresh coat of seal to see it through the winter.

If you prefer the natural colour change that occurs without seal you will need to remove any marks which appear with steel wool rubbed in the direction of the grain. If the colour is not to your liking you can lighten it with a proprietary wood bleach.

Never use creosote on garden chairs as it will come off on clothes.

Wood furniture that is left outside during winter should be stood on wood blocks so that the feet are not in constant contact with damp ground.

Cane must be brought indoors during winter, otherwise the bindings may rot from exposure to constant wet weather. A shed or garage is a suitable place to store it as a heat source will cause it to split. (See furniture, page 105.) Rub down and paint with clear polyurethane varnish to maintain appearance.

Plastic Clean with a solution of detergent or washing-up liquid, using an old toothbrush to get dirt out of cracks. Rinse well, using a hose if possible. Dry with old towels to prevent streaking and apply an aerosol polish to give some protection.

Cover-ups You will keep garden furniture cleaner if you protect it from adverse weather. You can buy plastic covers to fit all shapes from canopied swing seats to simple benches; but even if you use covers always store cushions and upholstery indoors.

Garden ornaments

Garden ornaments made from lead or stone need no cleaning.

Marble should be cleaned with a solution of household soap and water plus 60ml ammonia to the bucketful. Swab with a clean soft cloth but note that this will remove any polish, so if you want a shine the marble will need to be repolished (see Addresses).

Garden tools

After use, either push tools through a pile of sand to remove the dirt, or scrape off as much mud as possible (it may be easier if you leave the dirt to dry first). Store with cutting edges and prongs off the ground and at the end of the gardening season clean all tools throughly and apply a coating of machine oil to keep them in good condition through the winter.

Lawn mowers If electric, remove from the electricity supply before cleaning. Use a piece of stick or bamboo cane to scrape off grass and dirt, clean out the air filter and clean and sharpen the blades. Oil non-electric mowers according to the manufacturer's instructions.

Garden tubs and window boxes

Terracotta and porous stone should be hosed with clear water; plastic and painted finishes can be scrubbed with a solution of household detergent. Rinse interiors thoroughly before replacing, or renewing, compost.

Ponds should only be cleaned out if there is evidence of disease in fish or plants or if there is so much vegetation that the pond is choked with débris.

Ponds

First decide what you are going to do with any fish or plants while cleaning is in progress. They should be kept in their existing water, perhaps in a child's paddling pool or other safe container. Cover with netting to keep out pets.

Drain the pond completely. Some old concrete ponds have plugs; otherwise you will have to syphon out the water to lower ground with a hose or pump, or bale it out, and scoop out any débris. If it has a liner, take great care not to puncture it either with sharp tools or with your shoes.

When the pond is clean, fill it up with rain or tap water; leave overnight for the chlorine in the tap water to evaporate. Trim back any plants which have got too big and replant them in aquatic plant pots containing clay soil or special compost. Return the fish to the pond in plastic bags of the water in which they have been resting. Leave the bags suspended in the new water for an hour or so until both water temperatures are the same; then release them.

Filtering removes dirt, and chemicals are used to oxidise bacteria. Your pool supplier or installer will be able to advise you on the appropriate products suitable for the filtration system of your pool. Skimming fallen leaves off the surface with a small fishing net on a long stick will stop these being sucked into the traps and clogging up the filtration system.

Swimming pools

There are machines which will 'vacuum' the base and sides of the pool automatically and these are certainly less back-breaking than doing the job manually with a brush on a handle.

Tombstones   If a family tombstone has become covered with moss and lichen, so that any inscription or design is illegible, take care with cleaning. Tombstones are made from a number of different types of stone, some of which are very porous and easy to damage. Use a bucket of soapy water and a soft-bristled brush to scrub gently.

If the growth is so bad that a chemical solution is needed, take advice from a monumental mason, as chemicals react in different ways on different types of stone.

CARS

Keeping your car clean helps maintain its value as well as ensuring it looks good.

Exteriors   Car bodywork can be cleaned either in an automatic car wash or by hand. A car wash will shampoo the bodywork and apply a coating of wax but will not get into any crannies or dirt traps and will not polish chrome.

By hand you can do a better job, though it will take time and effort. Use a hose or buckets of water to remove mud and grit. Make sure before you start that all doors and windows and the sunroof are tightly closed.

Next, use a grit-free cloth and a bucket of detergent solution to wash over the whole of the car's bodywork, starting with the roof and working down. Alternatively you can use a proprietary car-washing kit consisting of a soft brush on the end of a hose which syphons water up from a bucket into the brush head.

Remove traces of tar with neat white spirit applied on a soft cloth.

washing kit consisting of a soft brush on the end of a hose which syphons water up from a bucket into the brush head.

Remove traces of tar with neat white spirit applied on a soft cloth.

Polishing is not essential but helps to protect the metal. Some polishes can be dissolved in a bucket of water and poured over the metal; they may dry shiny or need to be buffed with a chamois leather. Others are applied by hand.

Chrome just needs washing over and rubbing with a dry cloth. If you choose to apply a chrome polish make sure that it is well rubbed in, otherwise it will come off on people's hands.

Any rust spots should be treated with a rust inhibitor, then touched up with the correct colour car paint.

Windows and windscreens should be cleaned with a chamois leather wrung out of a bucket of soapy water. Rinse and polish well to avoid streaking. You can buy a special brand of glass protector which puts a dirt-resisting layer over the glass and keeps it cleaner for longer, particularly in muddy or dusty conditions. (See Directory of Brand Names.)

Interiors

Remove all rubbish from the car floor and the ashtrays, then use the attachments on your vacuum cleaner to get into nooks and crannies where dust and dirt accumulate. If you do not have a garage with a power point you will need either an extension lead or a small, battery-run vacuum cleaner. Use a spray cleaner and polish on the dashboard, glove compartment and any other hard surfaces.

If the upholstery is leather, wipe it with a damp cloth which has been rubbed over a tablet of glycerine soap. Do not rinse as the glycerine helps keep leather soft. Occasionally apply a little hide food to maintain suppleness but make sure it is rubbed in well and will not come off on people's clothes.

BICYCLES

These need cleaning little and often so that dirt does not build up on the frame or moving parts. Lubricate moving parts with a light, Teflon-based oil (see Part 11, Directory of Brand Names), once or twice a week. These oils do not attract dirt in the way a heavy oil does.

Clean the chain and sprockets with paraffin applied on a toothbrush for the chain and a 3-inch paintbrush (which should fit neatly between the sprockets). Clean the gear mechanism using paraffin on a 1-inch paintbrush. To clean the frame use a solution of washing-up liquid; work up a good lather, then rinse off. Do not use a hosepipe as the powerful jet of water could wash out the bearings, which are close to the surface. Dry with a soft cloth and just before everything is dry spray the moving parts with light oil. Keep oil away from the brake pads and the rims of the wheels.

Protect leather saddles from the wet by tying a plastic bag over them. Give the saddle an occasional coating of saddle soap to keep it soft and protect it. Vinyl saddles just need wiping with a damp cloth.

7

PETS AND PESTS

Animals and hygiene

Cats and dogs

Small pets

Caged birds

Fish

Household pests

Insects in the home

ANIMALS AND HYGIENE

There is probably some truth in saying if you want to keep your home spotless, do not keep pets. While they can bring lots of pleasure to their owners, they also shed hairs, sleep on furniture and never wipe their feet!

Uninvited creatures can do more serious damage. Mice, rats and invasions of insects can all wreak havoc in your home. It is sometimes necessary to call in the authorities to get rid of them.

CATS AND DOGS

The main problem is the hairs they shed. You can buy special gadgets for removing pet hairs from upholstery and carpets where a vacuum cleaner has not succeeded but an equally successful solution is to wrap sticky tape (Sellotape, masking tape) round your fingers – sticky-side out – and attack affected areas. Replace the tape as it becomes clogged up with hairs.

Regular grooming of the animal(s) will remove loose hairs and entangled débris. The earlier in their lives you start grooming them, the less they will resent it.

Bath dogs when necessary; those fond of rolling in smelly matter will require frequent bathing. It is possible to bath cats if you get them used to it from an early age, but on the whole they are good at grooming themselves.

Try to train cats and dogs to sleep in one place (not easy!) on bedding which can be washed. There is no need to buy anything special – old jumpers, worn blankets or picnic rugs make perfectly good bedding. Just remember to wash it regularly.

Cats and dogs are easily house-trained as long as you do it when they are young.

Walk your dog regularly and make sure it performs somewhere suitable (some councils provide special areas for dogs' excreta) or take a poop scoop and plastic bag with you so you can clear up any mess.

For cats the best solution if possible is to fit a cat flap so that they can attend to matters outdoors. If not, or in the event of your cat being ill, provide a litter tray. You will get less smell around the house if you use one which has a 'lid' and looks rather like a small dog kennel. The litter tray must be cleaned out daily. Use hot water and a little disinfectant, then rinse thoroughly. Provide fresh litter every day.

If your house smells strongly and unacceptably of cat or dog ask your vet to recommend a deodorising product, but be careful where you spray it – some may affect carpets or upholstery. As always, test on a small inconspicuous area first.

Cat fleas can also become a household problem. To clear your home of fleas invest in some flea spray or powder. First spray some of it inside your vacuum cleaner bag so that any live fleas or pupae collected by it are killed. Then vacuum thoroughly all around the house, using tools such as the crevice attachment to get into nooks and crannies. Also vacuum any furniture on which the cat has slept, including beds.

Treat the cat or dog with flea spray at the same time as cleaning the house. Most flea sprays are toxic so use it out of doors, following the manufacturer's instructions for application.

Flea products are available from pet shops and some chemists but you will get a stronger, more effective (and more expensive) brand from your vet which is likely to work better. You can try once a cat is clear of fleas to get it to wear a flea collar, but unfortunately cats can pick up fleas anywhere at any time and you should be prepared to deal with the problem on a regular basis.

A pill has been developed to prevent flea infestation. After the cat has eaten it, it develops a substance in the blood stream which prevents fleas reproducing themselves. Ask your vet for advice on whether your pet needs it.

If the flea infestation is too bad for you to treat yourself call in a pest control contractor.

SMALL PETS

Gerbils, hamsters and mice need to be kept scrupulously clean if their cages are kept indoors or they will smell, and the animals will be disturbed by their unhygienic environment.

Change bedding regularly, together with whatever you use for the floor of the cage. You should clean the toilet area daily and the material in the sleeping area once or twice a week.

Those animals such as guinea pigs and rabbits whose hutches are generally outdoors need less frequent attention, although they too should be kept in hygienic and comfortable conditions.

Once a month clean all hutches and cages thoroughly. Take out everything and wash and dry the area. Make sure you have somewhere safe to put the pet while this is going on.

CAGED BIRDS

Daily cleaning is needed to remove droppings, seed husks, any uneaten matter and moulted feathers. The easiest way to get rid of them is to line the base of the cage with old newspaper and a layer of sand which collects the droppings and can just be slid into a disposal bag.

Once a week clean the cage thoroughly. If your bird(s) have an exercise period each day, do the cleaning while they are flying. Otherwise find somewhere safe for them – a cat's wicker travelling basket is useful.

Remove all the bits and pieces in the cage and wash and dry it. Check any toys, mirrors and so on for cracks or sharp edges and remove anything that is damaged.

Wipe over the inside of the cage with damp kitchen paper, including the perches. Check whether the perches have become too smooth and, if so, use sandpaper to give a rough surface for the bird's feet.

If you have an aviary the cleaning procedure is the same but will be more onerous because of the larger number of birds involved. Use a stiff broom to wash down concrete floors. If the floor is bare earth, rake off as much of the droppings as you can.

FISH

Cold-water fish should be cleaned out when their tank starts to look silted up. Some types are dirtier than others and need more frequent cleaning. Put out bowls of water some hours before you clean the tank so that it reaches room temperature and some of the chlorine can evaporate. Just before you clean it catch the fish (you can buy a small soft net at aquatic retailers) and put them into one of the bowls, making sure that it is sufficiently deep for them not to leap out.

Remove the pebbles or gravel from the base of the tank and wash under running water until all slime and algae have gone. A metal colander makes a good container for this as it stops small pieces of gravel slipping down the plughole and blocking the waste outlet.

Scrub off the deposit that has formed on the sides of the tank. Rinse any live weed and replace it if it looks past its best.

Return the gravel to the tank, reposition weed and ornaments, fill up and return the fish to it. With open-topped tanks, keeping the water level up will keep the fish cleaner.

Tropical fish require the same cleaning procedure but it is essential that, while out of the tank, the fish are kept in heated water. Cleaning out tropical fish tanks is a job best done by two people – one to do the dirty work and the other to keep boiling kettles of water (a bit like home midwifery) and checking the temperature of the water in which the fish are stored. With even a smallish tank the cleaning procedure can take some time.

When cleaning out the fish tank watch out for your cat, which may be able to get at the fish in their bowl.

Pets, especially local dogs and cats, can do damage to gardens. Apply an aerosol pet deterrent to fences, doorways, gateposts, window boxes, dustbins and plant stems. Aerosols should remain effective for a few days in dry weather.

HOUSEHOLD PESTS

Mice enjoy the warmth and shelter of buildings and are not fazed by human company. They can cause   *Mice* damage to the structure of a home because of their need to nibble, which can destroy electric cables, gas and water pipes. If they get near food they will contaminate it and they carry a number of diseases, including food poisoning.

Mouse traps are suitable only if you do not have a large colony in the house. Otherwise it is best to call in the pest control unit. Mice have become immune to many of the over-the-counter poisons you can buy and those provided by pest control agencies are stronger. Once the mice have been disposed of, block up holes with wire wool and quick-setting cement.

Pigeons   Pigeons can transmit diseases to humans and are very dirty birds. If they have found a way into your loft, the local authorities are able to deal with them, so contact your local environmental health department.

Rats   Rats, oddly enough, are easier to get rid of than mice and less keen on domestic environments, preferring sewers and rubbish dumps. Like mice, they chew things and will damage the structure of a home and also spread disease and food poisoning. To get rid of them either buy rat poison or call in pest control experts.

Do not allow the problem to escalate once you have discovered mice or rats.

Squirrels   Squirrels like the warmth and comfort of domestic lofts and cause both damage and noise once they move in. They love to eat the casing on electrical cable, and will make nests out of loft insulation material. You cannot kill them yourself since they require a strong pesticide which can only be used by people trained under the Control of Pests Regulations (1986).

Once you have called in the experts and they have returned to pick up any dead animals, make sure no bodies are left which could decay and smell, then block up the eaves, using chicken wire so that air can still circulate in the area.

INSECTS IN THE HOME

You need first to find their nest; watch where they move when they are carrying food. Pour a kettle of boiling water over the nest, then puff an insecticidal powder into the hole. Paint insecticidal lacquer around their most frequently used door thresholds and where the floor meets the wall.

Ants

Carpet beetles damage carpets and bedding by biting the threads in them. You need an appropriate insecticide to kill the larvae and beetles, and damaged items should also be sprayed with a carpet beetle control product.

Carpet beetles (woolly bears)

To prevent their return, check you have no old birds' nests or dead birds in the loft or under the eaves. Vacuum the shelves and floors in your airing cupboard, and lift carpets and underlay to vacuum the floor below.

These not only ruin clothes but can damage carpets and upholstery. Be careful how you store woollens and fur coats, which are favourite breeding grounds. If you are storing them away, put a sachet of moth-repellent in with them.

Clothes moths

Keep your loft free of unused fabric or carpet, and at the first sign of moths, spray upholstery, carpets and clothes with mothproofer.

Cockroaches carry various diseases including food poisoning. They are nocturnal and will eat almost anything. Use an aerosol insecticide for cockroaches, but if this fails contact the environmental health department of your local authority.

Cockroaches

Fleas See page 167.

Flies These transmit food poisoning and other diseases. Be scrupulously clean in the kitchen and do not leave refuse lying around. Keep the lids on bins, and clean them out frequently. Spray the inside with insecticide. Keep food covered or refrigerated at all times. If flies are a real problem, invest in an ultra-violet electric flykiller of the type seen in some food shops. Remember that one teaspoon of waste left lying around will feed 200 houseflies!

> **Store pesticides out of reach of children and people with poor eyesight. Follow the instructions exactly.**

8

CLEANING IN SPECIAL CIRCUMSTANCES

Fire and flood damage

Infectious diseases and illness

Cleaning for the less able

Babies in the home

FIRE AND FLOOD DAMAGE

Professional help is usually needed after a fire or a flood, but there is action you can take beforehand to minimise the damage to your home – and your bank balance.

First and foremost, be sure that you are fully and correctly insured in the event of damages, so that you can replace everything that is lost. The building itself should be insured for the rebuilding cost, not its market value. If you are insured on a 'new for old' policy, you will be able to replace damaged items with new ones (this may exclude clothing). Insurance on an 'indemnity basis' means that the insurers will make a reduction for wear and tear on the items before they were damaged, and this may mean you are unable to replace them. Bear in mind too that your insurers can insist on certain items being cleaned and repaired rather than replaced. Most household policies do not cover damage to fences and gates.

Before winter comes, check roofs, chimneys and gutters, clear drain gratings and repair any damaged fences and walls.

Frozen and burst pipes If a pipe has frozen, turn off the main stop valve. Thaw the pipe, using a hair-dryer, hot water bottle or towel soaked in very hot water, along the pipe's length from the tap end towards the tank. Turn off the boiler and call in a plumber.

If a pipe bursts, again turn off the stop valve. If the burst is on a pipe leading from a storage tank, try to prevent all the water escaping. If you cannot stop the flow, turn on all the cold taps in the house. Turn off the central heating and any immersion heaters and call a plumber.

Flooding If you have any advance warning of flooding in your area, move as many of your possessions off the ground floor as possible. Put sandbags along the bottoms of doors and over air bricks. Do not use electricity or gas or draw off any tap water until the authorities say it is safe to do so. If your home is flooded, lift floor coverings so they will dry more quickly. Wash walls and floors in a disinfectant

solution and leave doors, windows and built-in cupboards open.

Remember that drying-out can take months, so
do not redecorate immediately. To avoid dry rot,
allow at least six months before re-laying floor
coverings.

> **Do not start any remedial work after fire or
> flood damage until the insurance company's
> loss adjuster has assessed the damage.**

If a storm or heavy snowfall damages your roof, use   *Roof damage*
sheets of hardboard or plastic to keep out rain and
snow. Shovel any snow off the loft floor before it
melts and drips through the ceilings below. Check
gutters for blockages.

INFECTIOUS DISEASES AND ILLNESS

It is rare for a house to hold the danger of infection even if someone
living in it has been ill. However, if you are concerned that there may
be a problem and someone vulnerable, like a pregnant mother, will be
coming to your home, contact the environmental health department of
your local authority and discuss the problem with staff there.

In cases of diseases like TB (which are highly infectious) or the pres-
ence of an invalid with suppurating wounds, contact the infection control nurse at your local hospital, who will be able to give advice on any
related problems.

If someone in the household is incontinent and needs to wear pads
or has dressings which need to be disposed of, consult the environmental health department of your local authority about arrangements
for disposal. There is usually a special collection for which you will be
supplied with special disposal bags.

CLEANING FOR THE LESS ABLE

While cleaning may be more difficult and time-consuming if you are physically disabled it may still be possible if you invest in some of the aids available to make certain tasks easier.

The Disabled Living Foundation (see Addresses) has displays in branches around Britain and has a list of mail-order catalogues from which you can select items that would be useful.

These include holders for brushes, cloths and scouring pads, washing-up brushes on suction cups, dishcloth wringers and window-cleaning gadgets. There are also extending handles for brooms and brushes and telescopic wall mops. You can fit special trigger handles to aerosols to make them easier to use.

For laundry, using a wheeled trolley saves you having to bend and if your eyesight is poor you can get a Braille conversion for the knobs on your washing machine. There are even water-soluble bags for laundry which you can just put into the machine in one go.

You or any sick or disabled person in your household may be entitled to special services which give practical help with cleaning the home. The Chronically Sick and Disabled Persons Act 1970 gives you the right to practical help with cleaning services if you are:

- substantially and permanently handicapped
- blind or partially sighted
- deaf or hard of hearing
- mentally ill
- mentally handicapped.

Your local branch of Age Concern (see Addresses) will advise you on your entitlement and you may be eligible for a grant for equipment or help in making your home more cleaning-friendly.

BABIES IN THE HOME

You do not need to be over-protective of babies. The adage about a peck of dirt still holds good to some extent although you should obviously take great care over sterilising bottles and washing hands and work surfaces before preparing food. There is no need to provide a clinical environment since in due course a baby has to get to grips with the real world. It is however important for both babies and young children that you do not leave any cleaning products in a place where they could find them and eat or drink them. For advice on laundering nappies, see page 134.

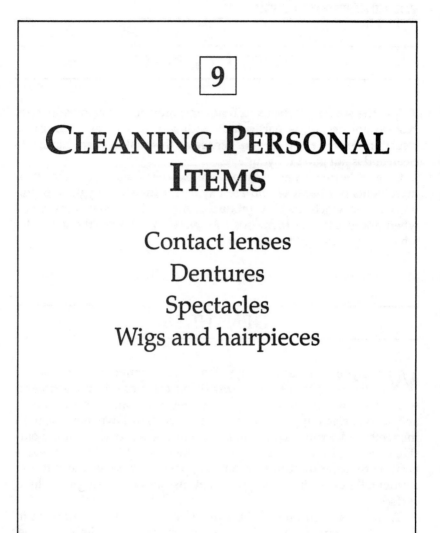

9

CLEANING PERSONAL ITEMS

Contact lenses
Dentures
Spectacles
Wigs and hairpieces

CONTACT LENSES

Use the special cleaner and fluids recommended by your optician. Do not use spit – particularly with soft lenses – as it can cause infection. Never sleep in your lenses as this makes them harder to clean and is not good for your eyes.

Contact lens-cleaning solutions are expensive not because of their ingredients but because you are paying for the strict hygiene conditions under which they are produced. Always keep containers closed when not in use, put them in a cool place and observe the date after which they should be thrown out.

DENTURES

While you can buy a range of denture cleaners and follow the instructions it is equally easy – and cheaper – to use soap and water. Fill a washbasin with tepid (not hot) water and use a nailbrush and soap to clean upper dentures. Use an up-and-down movement on the teeth and scrub carefully in between the areas that touch the outside cheek and palate and the gums. The reason for filling the washbasin is that the dentures become slippery as you clean and if you accidentally drop them they will float instead of breaking on a hard surface.

Clean lower dentures in the same way but avoid holding them in the palm of your hand, which may squeeze and snap the horseshoe. Dentures are fragile when not held in place by the jaw. Hold one side at a time as you work. Never use toothpaste as it will abrade the pink plastic and get rid of its high gloss. Also the scratching will make cleaning more difficult.

Clean dentures twice a day, otherwise calcium and tartar from the saliva will build up and you will need to pay for professional cleaning by a dentist.

SPECTACLES

It is important to clean spectacles regularly as a build-up of dirt interferes with the way light travels through the lenses. Special cloths, available from opticians, literally slice off the dirt. They are made from a special fibre which is long-lasting and washable.

To clean spectacles thoroughly, rinse them under cold or tepid running water, then in a solution of washing-up liquid. Rinse and wipe with a soft non-fluffy cloth. Do not use paper tissues as some brands contain particles of wood pulp which can scratch the lenses.

Many firms will clean your spectacles free of charge using an autosonic system which gets out the dirt which lodges between the lens and the frame.

If you have a greasy build-up on lenses you can use surgical or methylated spirit but take care not to get these chemicals on plastic frames or enamelled metal.

WIGS AND HAIRPIECES

Synthetic wigs should be cleaned in a solution of washing-up liquid or laundry detergent and left to dry naturally. Nowadays they do not melt under a hair-dryer (use the cool setting) but natural drying is recommended.

Machine-made human hair wigs should be cleaned with shampoo for normal hair followed by conditioner (essential, since natural oils from the head do not get into the hair). You can use a dryer to style them.

Hand-knotted human hair wigs made in the UK need to be cleaned with a special dry-cleaning fluid that is not available over the counter. You therefore need to use a specialist wig cleaner; wigs supplied on the National Health Service are cleaned once a month, free of charge (two wigs are supplied to those who need them); extra cleaning must be paid for and those who buy wigs themselves also need to find a cleaner. These wigs can be washed like human hair but must be blocked into position the minute shampooing is over. Do not use a polystyrene wig stand for this (although it is perfectly all right for normal off-the-head storage) but buy a cork and linen stand (see Addresses) which will support the wig while drying naturally. Because the hair is human it will move when wet and failure to block the wig correctly will mean it loses its style.

10

FIRST AID AND SAFETY

First aid for cleaning-related
accidents
Dealing with accidents and
emergencies

FIRST AID FOR CLEANING-RELATED ACCIDENTS

Some cleaning chemicals and activities are potentially hazardous. Prevention is always better than cure, so do protect yourself and others by taking note of the advice in this section.

Safety precautions

- Protect exposed areas of skin from coming into contact with chemicals. Wear heavy-duty rubber or plastic gloves (thin disposable gloves may be weakened by strong chemicals).
- Make sure no chemical, grit or sharp object gets into your eyes. Ordinary glasses provide some protection but safety goggles (from d-i-y shops) cover the whole area surrounding the eyes and are absolutely vital if you are doing something like scraping rust from metal window frames.
- Avoid breathing in unpleasant, possibly toxic, fumes. A face mask (from d-i-y shops) will help with this but it is also sensible to keep the room well-ventilated, opening as many doors and windows as you can.
- Never use any flammable product in an area where there is a naked flame, or electrical element – for example, an open or electric fire, a pilot light or an unextinguished cigarette. Deal with these before you start.
- Make sure electrical appliances are in good working order. Do not touch them, or electrical sockets, with wet hands. Use the correct fuse for the appliance.
- Do not take unnecessary risks. For example, never do work that involves standing on a ladder if you are alone. If you fall and injure yourself you could find it difficult to get help.
- Do not leave cleaning equipment lying around. It is all too easy to forget there is a bucket of dirty water behind a door as you breeze in with the vacuum cleaner. Clear up as you go along.

- Eliminate home hazards as far as possible. Secure loose rugs, mop up spills as they occur and do not over-polish floor surfaces, which could make them slippery.
- Keep all household cleaning products locked away if children or elderly people with poor eyesight are at large.
- Keep a basic first aid kit somewhere handy and replace any items which get used. Ensure other members of your household know where it is kept.

- sticking plasters – strips or shapes, fabric and waterproof, individually wrapped
- roll of microtape for securing dressings
- crêpe bandages
- triangular bandage for making a sling
- tweezers for getting out splinters
- blunt-ended scissors for cutting tapes, plasters and bandages to size
- safety-pins for securing bandage or sling
- antiseptic wipes
- paracetamol syrup for children, paracetamol/ aspirin for adults
- antiseptic disinfectant
- calamine lotion
- eyebath and eye wash
- sterile eye dressing.

A basic first aid kit

Keep all first aid items in a clearly marked box. Stick the number of your GP's surgery, local pharmacist and nearest accident and emergency department on the inside. If you are out at work and someone else is in your home – a childminder or cleaner – put your telephone number and that of a member of your family somewhere prominent.

Unless you are trained in first aid, keep a basic booklet on first aid procedures in the box as well.

DEALING WITH ACCIDENTS AND EMERGENCIES

ADMINISTERING ARTIFICIAL RESPIRATION

When someone stops breathing, brain damage can occur after three minutes. Use this technique to re-start breathing.
- Lie the person down.
- Using your hands on forehead and chin, tilt the head back to open up the windpipe and clear the air passage.
- Check the mouth for obstructions and remove anything you can clearly see. Leave false teeth in if they fit well.
- Keeping the head in the tilted position, pinch the nose between two fingers, place your lips over the person's mouth and blow in two long breaths to make the chest rise.
- Remove your mouth while the chest falls.
- Provided there is still a pulse, repeat this procedure every four or five seconds until breathing re-starts.

When this happens, put the patient in the recovery position, as follows:
- Place the person on his/her back.
- Tilt the head to open the airway.
- Place the arm nearest to you at right angles to the body, elbow bent, palm uppermost.
- Bring the other arm across and hold the hand against the chest.
- Grasp the thigh furthest from you and pull up the knee, keeping the foot flat on the ground.
- With the hand against the cheek, pull on the thigh to roll the person towards you, resting the head upon the outstretched hand.

- Tilt the head back to open the airway and adjust the hand under the cheek to ensure it stays open.
- Adjust the leg so that the hip and knee are at right angles.

Broken bones

Do not move the person. If a leg is broken (or you suspect this) call an ambulance; if it is an arm, take the person to hospital in a car using pillows or cushions to keep him/her in as stable a position as possible.

Burns and scalds

Unless a burn is minor, seek medical attention. Remove any jewellery near the burn or scald. Then cool it by holding the burn under running water for at least ten minutes, or until the pain lessens. This stops the burn from continuing to develop.

Cover the burn with a clean cloth or dry sterile dressing but do not apply any cream or lotion. If the burn is severe do not attempt to remove any clothing sticking to it.

Raise burned limbs above heart level to reduce the blood flow to them, and apply a series of cool compresses to reduce the 'cooking' effect. Dry and cover with a sterile dressing or clean cloth.

If clothing is on fire, lie the person down to keep flames away from the head. Wrap him/her up in a rug, blanket or piece of heavy fabric (curtain, coat) made from natural fibres – synthetics will stick to the burn. Pour water or other non-flammable liquid on the burn.

Cuts

If there is persistent bleeding lie the person down and remove clothing from around the cut. If possible, raise the cut above the level of the heart to reduce bleeding. If it is a straightforward cut with nothing embedded in it, cover with a piece of gauze and, holding the sides of the cut together, press down hard on it for 5-15 minutes. Add further layers of gauze or paper towel if blood comes through but do not remove the original ones. Bandage firmly in place. If bleeding continues, call an ambulance.

If something is embedded in the cut, do not remove it: it is acting as a plug. Cover the cut with clean cloth. Take two pieces of gauze and fold them into sausage shapes. Place on either side of the cut, then bandage them gently into position, taking care not to press on the embedded object. Take the person to your nearest accident and emergency department.

Electric shock Get the person away from the electrical appliance. First either remove the plug from the socket, holding the flex as you pull, or switch off the power at the mains. If neither is possible use a broom handle to push the person away from the electricity supply. Do not touch the person until he/she is away from the source of the shock. Call an ambulance. If necessary, administer artificial respiration (as above), then place the person in the recovery position.

Cool the burn either under a running tap or by applying a series of cold compresses.

Pat dry, then cover with a clean cloth (a pillow case) or dry sterile dressing.

Head injury Call an ambulance to take the person immediately to your nearest accident and emergency department.

Poişoning Call an ambulance straight away. If the person becomes unconscious ease him/her into the recovery position. If breathing stops, administer artificial respiration, as above.

If bleach has been drunk, give sips of milk or water to dilute it. Do not give any liquid if the person has swallowed a non-corrosive poison. Do not attempt to make the person vomit, which may in any case occur naturally. Collect a sample of the poison or its container and any vomit to give to the doctor.

Splinters Wash hands and sterilise the tweezers by holding them briefly in a flame or boiling them in water for ten minutes. Clean the area round the splinter with soap and warm water, taking care not to push it in further. Pat the area dry with a tissue and use the tweezers to remove the splinter, taking care not to break off the exposed bit so that it becomes impossible to remove. If your eyesight is bad use a magnifying glass.

Wash the area. Wait for any bleeding to stop, then cover with a plaster.

● If you fail to remove the splinter, go to the doctor. Do not assume it will work its way out of its own accord.

For a sprained ankle, first remove the shoes: if the person is wearing boots you may need to cut the boot away. Raise the ankle or wrist above the level of the person's head and apply a cold compress to the painful area. Bandage the sprain firmly, using a figure-of-eight pattern.

Sprained ankle or wrist

Raise the injury above the level of the person's head. Apply a cold compress.

Bandage firmly, but not so tightly that any swelling is impeded. If the injury is to an arm, the arm should be put in a sling.

Strains

11

DIRECTORY OF BRAND NAMES

This list is a guide to some of the many cleaning products currently available. Note that supermarkets and chemists produce a range of own-brand products which work well and may be cheaper than other brands. When you buy a product, check whether it has a use-by date and, if so, observe it.

Aerosol cleaners	*Dettox* *Flash* *Jif* *Mr Muscle*
Bath cleaners	*Ajax Cream Cleanser* *Izal Bath Cleaner* *Jenolite Bath Stain Remover* *Oz Bathroom Cleaner and Limescale Remover*
Carpet treatments	*Antron* *Scotchgard**
Carpet and upholstery shampoo	*Bissell* *Carpet Devils* *Kleeneze Carpet and Upholstery Shampoo* *1001*
Chandeliers	*Antiquax Chandelier Cleaner*
Chewing-gum remover	*Keyline Chewing Gum Remover** *Stain Devils Glue and Chewing Gum Remover**
Cleaner/ polishes	*Johnson's Wax Free Sparkle* *Mr Sheen*
Decanter dryer	*Manor House decanter dryer**
Descalers	*Ataka Bath Stain Remover and Kettle Descaler* *Descalite Kettle Scale Remover* *Melitte Quick Descaler* *Oz Iron Cleaner* *Scale Away*

Dettol *Milton*	***Disinfectant/*** ***sterilising*** ***products***
Antiquax Liquid Floor Wax *Cardinal Red Tile Polish* *Cardinal Self-Shine Red Liquid* *Dunlop Floor Polish* *Johnson's Traffic Wax** *Johnson's Wax Klear* *Johnson's Wax Free Sparkle* *Marley Floorgloss* *Rentokil Wax Polish* *Ronuk Lavender Wax*	***Floor polishes***
Cuprinol Interior Mould Killer *Dax Fungo* *Rentokil Mould Cure*	***Fungicidal*** ***wash***
Antiquax *Briwax* *Johnson's Wax Furniture Cream with Beeswax* *Lord Sheraton Furniture Balsam* *Mansion Enriched Cream* *Mansion Wax Polish* *Renaissance Wax Polish** *Stephenson Olde English Furniture Cream*	***Furniture*** ***polish***
Ajax Cream Cleanser *Bar Keeper's Friend* (rust and tarnish stains on brass, chrome, glass, marble, plastic) *Cleen-O-Pine* *Domestos Multi-surface liquid cleaner* *Ecover Cream Cleaner* *Flash liquid* *Jif*	***General*** ***cleaners***
*Clear-shield** *SOS Glass Works* *Windolene*	***Glass cleaners***
See chewing-gum remover, above.	***Glue remover***

Grout whiteners	New Look White Grout Reviver Polycell Versalite
Hide food	Connolly's Cee Bee hide food* Fortificuir
Lavatory cleaners	Domestos Fresh Harpic Limescale Remover Jeyes Sanilav Oz Toilet Descaler Vortex
Light oil	3-in-One Penetrating and Easing Oil
Lubricant	WD40
Marble, slate and stone cleaners	Bel Products*
Metal cleaners	Astonish Brasso Metal Polish Wadding Goddard's Long Term Brass and Copper Polish Goddard's Long Term Silver Polish Hagerty's Copper WashHagerty's Metal Polish Hagerty's Silver CleanHagerty's Silver Foam Solvol Autosol Tarnprufe silver storage bags* Town Talk Silver Foam Town Talk Silver Rinse
Mildew treatment	Mystox*
Net curtain whitener	Dylon Super White
Oven cleaners	Easy-Off Kleenoff Mr Muscle

Bissell 'Not on the Carpet' Accident Cleaner *Shaws No-Stain*	*Pet stain* *treatments*
Vanish	*Pre-wash* *products*
Astonish *Shiny Sinks*	*Scale removers*
Colron Ring Remover *Colron Scratch Remover* *Joy Scratch Dressing* *Liberon Burnishing Cream* *Liberon Wax Sticks* *Topps Scratch CoverTopps Ring-Away*	*Scratch* *and mark* *treatments*
Beaucaire *Dabitoff* *Goddard's Dry Clean* *K2r* *Manger's De-Solv-It* *Movol (rust)* *Thawpit* *The Stain Slayer*	*Stain* *removers*
Bal Ceramic Tile Cleaner *Rentokil Ceramic Tile Cleaner*	*Tile cleaners*
See carpet and upholstery shampoo, above.	*Upholstery* *cleaner*

* denotes that the product is obtainable only through one supplier, the address of which can be found in Part 12.

12

ADDRESSES

Many trade organisations operate a code of practice agreed with the Office of Fair Trading. When looking for a specialist cleaner it is advisable to choose a member of one of these organisations, if appropriate, since they are usually prepared to arbitrate if there is a dispute.

The symbol † below denotes trade organisation.

Antiques
British Antique Dealers' Association
20 Rutland Gate
London SW7 1BD
071-589 4128
Information on caring for antique carpets and rugs, clocks, furniture, prints, silver watercolours and paintings

†London and Provincial Antique Dealers Association Ltd
Suite 214
535 Kings Road
London SW10 0SZ
071-823 3511

Sothebys
34-35 New Bond Street
London W1A 2AA
071-493 8080

Asthma
The British Allergy Foundation
Freephone 0800 318385

Blinds
The British Blind and Shutter Association
Heath Street
Tamworth
Staffs B79 7JH
0827 52337
Advice on cleaning all types of blind

Books
The Antiquarian Booksellers' Association
Suite 2, 26 Charing Cross Road
London WC2H 0DG
071-379 3041
List of members that can clean and conserve old books

Carpets
†British Carpet Manufacturers' Association
Royalty House
72 Dean Street
London W1V 5HB
071-734 9853

British Carpet Technical Centre
Wira House
West Park Ring Road
Leeds LS16 6QL
0532 591999
Advice on technical problems with carpets

National Carpet Cleaners Association Ltd
126 New Walk,
De Montfort Street
Leicester LE1 7JA
0533 554352
Members required to maintain specified standards for cleaning carpets and upholstery and operate a code of practice covering fair pricing, service, complaints procedures, liability and consumer protection

Thames Carpet Cleaners
48-56 Reading Road
Henley-on-Thames
Oxon RG9 1AG
0491 574676
Advice on cleaning oriental carpets

Cars
†Society of Motor Manufacturers and Traders Ltd
Forbes House
Halkin Street
London SW1X 7DS
071-235 7000

Chimney cleaning
National Association of Chimney Sweeps
St Mary's Chambers
19 Station Road
Stone
Staffs ST15 8JP
0785 811732

Cleaning cloths
Vale Mill (Rochdale) Ltd
John Street
Rochdale LL16 H1R
Supplier of a wide range of Minky cloths for cleaning specific materials

Cleaning with disabilities
Age Concern England
Astral House
1268 London Road
London SW16 4ER
081-679 8000

Age Concern Northern Ireland
3 Lower Crescent
Belfast BT7 1NR
0232 245729

Age Concern Scotland
54a Fountainbridge
Edinburgh EH3 9PT
031-228 5656

Age Concern Cymru
1 Cathedral Road
Cardiff
CF1 9SD
0222 371566
Advice available from any of the above on help to which those with disabilities may be entitled

Chester-care
Sidings Road
Lowmore Industrial Estate
Kirkby-in-Ashfield
Notts NG17 7JZ
0623 757955
Mail order catalogue featuring useful cleaning aids

Disabled Living Foundation
380-384 Harrow Road
London W9 2HU
071-289 6111
Permanent display of equipment, some of which helps with cleaning, may be seen at this address and centres around Britain

Keep Able Store and Mail Order Division
Fleming Close
Park Farm Industrial Estate
Wellingborough
Northants NN8 6UF
0933 679426
Mail order catalogue

Condensation
Condensation Advisory Bureaux
PO Box 12
Yarm
Cleveland TS15 9YW
0388 450503
Advice on dealing with condensation problems

Cork
The Cork Industry Federation
62 Leavesden Road
Weybridge
Surrey KT13 9BX
0932 848416
Advice on care of cork finishes

Craftsmen
The Guild of Master Craftsmen
166 High Street
Lewes
East Sussex BN7 1XU
0273 478449
Register of members who can clean damaged craft items

Decanters
Hurley Style Ltd
The Manor House
Hurley
Berkshire SL6 5NB
0628 824303
Supplier of special decanter dryer containing moisture-absorbing crystals

Dry-cleaners
Brooks Services Group
210 Aztec West
Almondsbury
Bristol BS12 4SN
0454 614668

Elias Hand Finished Dry Cleaners
68 St Johns Wood St
London NW8 7SH
071-722 2212

Harry Berger
25 Station Road
Cheadle Hulme
Cheshire FK8 5AF
061-485 3421

Johnson Group Cleaners
Mildmay Road
Bootle
Merseyside L20 5EW
051-933 6161

Lakeland Pennine Group Plc
Abbey Road
Barrow-in-Furness
Cumbria LA14 1XL
0229 820800

Lewis & Wayne Ltd
9 Streatham High Road
London SW16 1DZ
081-769 8777

Master Services Group
Unit 4
Thornhill Industrial Park
Hope Street
Rotherham S60 1LH
0709 829771

All the above dry-cleaning companies have a number of branches capable of high-quality dry-cleaning of items such as designer evening wear, wedding dresses, antique christening robes and other valuable textiles or those which are of sentimental value

Enamelware
Vitreous Enamel Development Council
New House
High Street
Ticehurst
East Sussex TN5 7AL
0379 650340

Electrical appliances
†The Association of Manufacturers of Domestic Electrical Appliances (AMDEA)
Leicester House
8 Leicester Street
London WC2H 7AZ
071-437 0678

Floor polish
Consumer Advisory Service
Johnson Wax
Frimley Green
Camberley
Surrey GU16 5AJ
0276 63456

Footwear
†The British Footwear Manufacturers' Federation
Royalty House
72 Dean Street
London W1V 5HB
071-437 5573

SATRA Footwear Technology Centre
SATRA House
Rockingham Road
Kettering
Northants NN16 9JH
0536 410000

Fungicidal treatment
Dax
PO Box 119
Nottingham
0602 609996
Supplier of Fungo anti-fungal wash, Daxo Brass and Copper treatments and an acrylic lacquer for brass and copper

Furniture
†British Furniture Manufacturers Federation
30 Harcourt Street
London W1H 2AA
071-724 0851

¯urniture polish
Picreator Enterprises
44 Park View Gardens
Hendon
London NW4 2PN
081-202 8972
Supplier by mail of Renaissance micro-crystalline wax furniture polish

General cleaning products
Kleeneze Ltd
Martins Road
Hanham
Bristol BS15 3DY
0272 670861
Door-to-door suppliers of a wide range of cleaning products. Ask for an agent to call

Glass
Glass and Glazing Federation
44-48 Borough High Street
London SE1 1XB
071-403 7177
Information on cleaning all types of glass

Ritec Ltd
15 Royal London Estate
West Road
London N17 0XL
081-885 5155
Supplier of Clear-shield solution, which puts a protective film on glass

Insurance
The Association of British Insurers
51-55 Gresham Street
London EC2V 7HQ
071 600 3333
Free leaflets on coping with flood and fire damage

Laundry
Home Laundering Consultative Council
7 Swallow Place
London W1R 7AA
071-408 0020

Leather
Connolly Leather Ltd
Wandle Bank
Wimbledon
London SW19 1DW
Advice on caring for leather

Marble
A. Bell & Co
Kingsthorpe Works
Kingsthorpe Road
Northampton NN2 6LT
0604 712505
Advice on caring for marble

Mildew
Picreator Enterprises
(see above under furniture polish)
Supplier by mail of a mildew treatment, Mystox

Motorcycles
Motor Cycle Industry Association Ltd
Starley House
Eaton Road
Coventry CV1 2FH
0203 227427

Outdoor clothing
Nikwax
Unit 4
Durgates Industrial Estate
Wadhurst
East Sussex TN5 6DF
0892 783855
Reproofing of outdoor wear, such as Goretex

Paintings and pictures
Association of British Picture Restorers
Station Avenue
Kew
Surrey TW9 3QA
081-948 5644

Pest control
The British Pest Control Association
3 St James Court
Friar Gate
Derby
Derbyshire DE1 1ZU
0332 294288
List of recommended specialist pest control contractors

Rentokil
Felcourt
East Grinstead
West Sussex
RH19 2JY
0342 833022

Pianos
Heckscher & Co
75 Bayham Street
London NW1 0AA
071-387 1735
*Suppliers of a range of cleaning products for pianos including key polishes,
Konig Polish Cleaner for polyester-finished cases and Konig Refresher for
french-polished cases*

Plastics
British Plastics Federation
6 Bath Place
Rivington Street
London EC2A 3JE
071-457 5000

Range cookers
Aga-Rayburn
PO Box 30
Ketley Telford
Shropshire TF1 4DD
0952 642000
Advice on cleaning range cookers

Silver storage
The Tarnprufe Co
68 Nether Edge Road
Sheffield S7 1RX
0742 553652
Supplier of bags and cutlery rolls for storing silver and silver-cleaning mitts

Stain removers
The Beckmann Stain Advisory Service
Dendron Ltd
Watford
Herts WD1 7JJ
Supplier of a wide range of Stain Devil products for specific stains. Write for advice

Mykal Industria
Farnsworth House
5 Morris Close
Park Farm Industrial Estate
Wellingborough
Northants NN8 6XF
0933 402822
Supplier of Manger's De-Solv-It

Textiles
Blicking Textile Conservation
Blicking Hall
Aylsham
Norwich NR11 6NF
0263 733471

Lakeland Plastics Ltd
Alexandra Buildings
Windermere
Cumbria LA23 1BQ
05394 88200
Supplier of net bags for delicate items which need machine-washing. Also net racks for drying items flat

Lever Brothers Ltd
Lever House
3 St James's Road
Kingston-upon-Thames
Surrey KT1 2BA
081-541 8200

Procter & Gamble Ltd
PO Box 1EL
New Sandgate House
City Road
Newcastle upon Tyne NE99 1EL
091-235 4000

Royal School of Needlework
Apartment 12a
Hampton Court Palace
East Molesey
Surrey KT8 9AU
081-943 1432
Cleaning and repair of embroidery and needlework

The Textile Conservation Centre
Apartment 22
Hampton Court Palace
East Molesey
Surrey KT8 9AU
081-977 4943
Advice on the conservation of valuable textiles

Textile Services Association Ltd
7 Churchill Court
58 Station Road
North Harrow
Middx HA2 7SA
081-863 7755/9177
Address list for specialist dry-cleaners and laundries

Wigs
A. H. Iles Ltd
146 Lower Road
London SE16 2UG
071-237 1422
Supplier of cork and linen blocks essential for cleaning certain types of wig

C. Raoul
34 Craven Road
London W2 3QA
071-723 6914
Wig cleaner and supplier

METRIC AND IMPERIAL MEASUREMENTS

Length			Volume		
Centimetres		*Inches*	*Litres*		*Gallons*
2.540	1	0.394	4.546	1	0.220
5.080	2	0.787	9.092	2	0.440
7.620	3	1.181	13.638	3	0.660
10.160	4	1.575	18.184	4	0.880
12.700	5	1.969	22.730	5	1.100
15.240	6	2.362	27.276	6	1.320
17.780	7	2.756	31.822	7	1.540
20.320	8	3.150	36.368	8	1.760
22.860	9	3.543	40.914	9	1.980

			Weight		
Metres		*Yards*	*Kilograms*		*Pounds*
0.914	1	1.094	0.454	1	2.205
1.829	2	2.187	0.907	2	4.409
2.743	3	3.281	1.361	3	6.614
3.658	4	4.374	1.814	4	8.819
4.572	5	5.468	2.268	5	11.023
5.486	6	6.562	2.722	6	13.228
6.401	7	7.655	3.175	7	15.432
7.315	8	8.749	3.629	8	17.637
8.230	9	9.843	4.082	9	19.842

Weight (solid)

1 oz	= 28 grams
1 pound	= 454 grams
1 stone	= 6.3 kilograms
1 cwt	= 50.8 kilograms

100 grams	= 3½ oz
200 grams	= 7 oz
1 kilogram	= 2 lbs 3 oz
1 tonne	= 0.9842 ton

Length

1 inch	= 2.5 centimetres
1 foot	= 30 centimetres
1 yard	= 91 centimetres
1 mile	= 1,609 metres

1 centimetre	= 0.4 inches
1 metre	= 3 yards 3 inches
1 kilometre	= 1,093 yards
1 kilometre	= 0.6214 mile

INDEX